COMPASS SEASON

FIND YOUR BEARINGS THROUGH NATURE'S INSPIRATION.

J. BRAGSTAD

Publisher's Cataloging the publication
John Bragstad

Compass Season: Find Your Bearings Through Nature's Inspiration - 1st ed.

ISBN 978-0-9996854-1-9

Quantity discounts are available to your company, writing organization or educational institution for academic purposes, subscription incentives, gifts or fundraising campaigns.

For more information, please contact Birch River Books at P.O. 248, Grand Marais, MN 55604 or email the author at:

birchriverbooks.mn@gmail.com

Please Note:

The content of this book is for information purposes and should **not** be construed as advice. If you are seeking help, consult with a professional therapist who can tailor treatment to your individual needs.

To my family: we've shared so many campsites,
from Nova Scotia and Newfoundland
to the Yukon.

Matthew, Allison and especially Susan,
I thank you, more than I can say.

CONTENTS

Introduction   vii

WEST: AUTUMN SHADOW

1. The Stalking Moon   3
2. Reaching for the Light   9
3. Shoulder Season   13
4. Hypothermia: Nature's Warning   19
5. Woodshed   27
6. Days of Brazen Color   33
7. Superior: First Light   37
8. Forest Undercover   43
9. Rivers Run Dry   47
10. Chik-Wauk   51

NORTH: WINTER COLD

1. The Ensuing Darkness   61
2. Unfound Riches   67
3. I Go Up To The North Country To Feel Small   73
4. Raw Beauty   77
5. Dawning Imperatives   81
6. Snow Buntings   87
7. Whispers   93
8. Northern Christmas   99
9. Arctic Sun   103
10. Spring Wait   107

EAST: SPRING'S ARRIVAL

1. The Ice Fields of March   115
2. The Invisible Hand   121
3. April Snow   127
4. Base Camps   131
5. Stars   137
6. Milestones   141
7. Split Rock: A Tribute to Those Who Are Aware   147
8. The Expectancy of the Day   151
9. The Laurentian Divide   155
10. Joy in Common Things   161

SOUTH: SUMMER WARMTH

1. Switchbacks   167
2. Kairos Time   171
3. Breaking Camp   177
4. Long Portages on Hot Days   181
5. Solstice   187
6. Watchfires   191
7. Unintended Consequences   195
8. The Coming of More   199
9. Blueberry Harvest   205
10. The Mysterious   209

ENDNOTES   215
Acknowledgments   229
Birch River Books   231
Book Clubs   233
Resources   235
About the Author   239

INTRODUCTION

Compass Season is a book that can be happily read from start to finish and digested entirely in that fashion. It's also the type of book that can slide off the couch on a Tuesday morning, and open to an article which magically speaks to the very real drama you find yourself in at that moment.

Just as Robert Frost spies the "something white" deep in the well, John Bragstad speaks on the spirituality and humanity represented by the landscape, and our interactions with it.

I was fortunate to spend some lovely dark winter evenings with John as we edited this book together. During these sessions, he would read aloud many of these passages, often in their entirety. And I got actually to hear how these words are to be read: softly, slowly and, at times, whispered. Like walking through the forest with a dear friend.

So read these words slowly, and don't be afraid to whisper them out loud as you read along. And don't be afraid, also, to let this wonderful book slide off the couch and magically open from time to time to speak to you directly!

Thomas Stamps, M.D.

I wrote this book for entirely selfish reasons. I wanted to recapture, back in my city life, what I had experienced in the wilds.

My childhood was spent vacationing in the cabin country of central Minnesota. It wasn't until I experienced the raw, untrammeled tapestry of the Boundaries Waters Canoe Area that I came alive to the wonders of nature. Before this, I had glimpses. Now, it was a buffet that had been set before me.

I wrote to preserve these memories, much like the person who takes a photograph. As I attempted to describe my experiences, other thoughts intruded.

I began to learn more about life, my life. I realized nature was not merely this inert place I was traveling through. Instead, it was my teacher, and it provided me with all sorts of new perspectives on routine and unimaginative thinking.

Some authors and poets had a profound effect on my writing. They broke from the bounds of pure travelogues to write about mystery and a wilderness ethic, the joy of knowing silences, the rhythmic chatter of chipmunks set against the tremolo laughter of loons.

These writers gave me both the courage and inspiration to allow nature to seep into my reflections and everyday thinking.

> I've learned much about how the winter solstice brings hope. There is a generosity to nature that flings wildflower seeds everywhere. Birds that survive the winter night are now more than a curiosity to me.

As a counselor, I would occasionally read some of these passages to those who would visit my office if I thought they would apply. They would often quiet busy and overly-complicated minds. They might shift that person's thinking.

These articles were the stuff that would take them from current problems to places where, for at least moments, the wild birds would sing.

It was my deeper satisfaction when people would take what I had written to extend it to something in their own lives and then, they would make it their own.

Perhaps that is what will happen to you. Whether you enjoy nature or not, these are metaphors you might find helpful in your journey. They might point you to truths you intuitively know.

As moonlight opens up the world again to the wilderness traveler, so might these extend what you can see and cast a singular beauty all their own.

Compasses give us the lay of the land.
They orient us to the maps before us.
They steady us when we are lost.

They guide us in unfamiliar territory.
They make adventure possible.

When satellite signals fade,
they are there to take us home.

J. Bragstad

WEST: AUTUMN SHADOW

Here I belong, but the green weeks fly.
And Autumn's brown fingers are painting the glen.
Answer me wild geese arrowing high,
How can I live in the town again?

Irene Stanley as transcribed from
Distant Fires (Scott Anderson)

ONE

THE STALKING MOON

The whitethroat started its long thin note bravely, then stopped in the middle as though suddenly realizing it wasn't daylight after all, but only the light of the moon.

Listening Point
Sigurd Olson

It is that time of year for anticipation. The long shadows are beginning to be noticed. The moon seems colder. Daylight is diminishing, and the waves out on the lake are more pewter and steel than only a few short weeks ago.

It is the time of waiting. Aboriginal people ascribe to the seasons words like Wild Rice Moon (August), Sucker Fish Moon (February), Freezing Over Moon (November), Sap Boiling Moon (April).

Here in the North, among the Ojibway, I'm told there

are other moons: the Crust on the Snow Moon (March), the Flower Budding Moon (May), the Strawberry Moon (June).

For me, October is the Stalking Moon. Winter carefully, quietly stalks those of us who stay in the North. The blush of fresh raspberries is gone. Leaves are losing their battle with the winds. Occasionally, there is the fire of maple but, for the most part, the world is muted with soft golds and browns.

"There's snow in Duluth today. Can you believe it?" is the first indication winter draws closer. For some it is joyful and to be tasted. I have grandchildren where, if I see snow, they see skiing.

For some, it is readiness. Getting the chimney swept of creosote, putting a sharp edge on the chainsaw, removing the strands of garden that will complicate things in the spring, these are what matter. These give the precambrian country its unique character.

Here, we wait knowing the first snow will change everything. We tell ourselves it won't last, but we are living on marginalized time. Soon, nature's patience will run out, and we will be encased in winter, as temperatures drop and frozen lakes accept nature's verdict.

OCTOBER IS the month of eagerness. In the spring, there are the long-delayed periods of time where ice and snow waltz with open ground. But now, in autumn, it often seems life is building to a crescendo. The geese have long since left, their perfect V formation cresting the trees. Wolves have put on their winter coats. Bears are denning in preparation for what is to come.

And winter arrives with grand pronouncement. In the city, we are accustomed to noise and inconvenience. The coming of snow brings more trouble managing life. It is a bothersome footnote to our busy days.

But I remember another late autumn morning when I was falling timber by myself at Seagull Lake. In the stillness nature held its breath, waiting for the curtain to rise. Then, winter came. That was the day when, like Black Cats, the fireworks of the new season appeared.

I was taking a break, straddling a large pine that had fallen the winter before. Suddenly, from all around, the ground was a snare drum of sound with ice crystals on fallen leaves. I could see a swirl of flurries coming in from across the lake. The silence was broken as a new guest announced its arrival.

In some ways, the island was the same, but now everything was changing. I knew I had better hurry. I thought it might already be too late if snows deepened and impeded my ability to move about so easily.

The Stalking Moon had found me, and winter was now an inevitability. While the ground was not yet blanketed with white, it was a harbinger of things to come.

The open paths skirting the camp, the pungent smell of

damp leaves, the playfulness of the waves cresting against the dock were soon to be gone. Even my hands, whether I was imagining it or not, seemed colder.

Don Ian Smith, one of my favorite authors, wrote about this steady march of the season in one of his books describing the high country of the Marshall Wilderness and the Salmon River of western Idaho.

In one of his chapters, he describes seeing a dusting of snow along the flank of one of these high mountain ranges. Even though he was down below on the flatlands, this was a signal, an early warning that before long life would be different. While things seemed the same and familiar, the frost and cold would soon visit him. He would come to know the deep drifts of snow filling his corrals and pastureland.

How often do we see this where, as with nature, we can glimpse our first sign and know it is the Anticipatory Moon, the Stalking Moon, that will not leave us alone for long? Such moments can almost be indistinguishable from all the cacophony around us if we are not paying attention.

Or if we ignore such signs. We can tell ourselves such moments will not come our way. However, the "snow in the high country" tells us of a different story.

The Boundary Waters Canoe Area of Minnesota, one of the grandest wilderness environments in the United States, is experiencing a Stalking Moon right now. Mining is encroaching on her borders. What will come of this? Who knows, but we must do what we can to prepare.

There is an even more subtle pressure. Those who visit this place are becoming older. Many of this generation can appreciate the rarity of this extraordinary experience. However, their voices are fewer. What will happen when the celebration of water and wind is lost to the confines of ease and a more virtual way of living?

This summer I heard a story about a young boy who was taken by his father to one of these magnificent lakes where the fishing was remarkable. Many times, the dad had thought about what it would be like to share this memory with his son. The joy and delight came home to him as he thrilled to his boy boating a three-pound pickerel.

"What did you think of that!" said the dad, more excited than inquisitive.

His son's answer: "Dad, I can do more in 10 minutes with my video fishing game than I can do here in a whole afternoon."

For what was to be a great bonding experience, how can moments such as this be comparable to a 10-pound video substitution? For some, who are removed from actual experience, is not this snow on the mountain?

IF WE THINK about our lives, I know the Stalking Moon is waiting for us as well.

It is a time of year we don't necessarily welcome. But we would be foolish to ignore it. It is a precursor to many changes where we will either adapt or suffer for it.

This moon often will delay as it forms. It gives us time to get ready. It does not visit itself on us all at once. Days of fleeting cold can be modulated by days of warmth when we are given far more than we expect or sometimes even deserve.

We ask for one more day, only this time of year we are

not at all sure nature will hear us. Sometimes we think we have gotten away with quite enough.

Some will venture into the parks, make camp along the streams, find themselves in trail-tested canoes with lively, energetic spirits ignoring the wind and dampness and the possibility of waking to snow. To be alone. To fish. To camp. To enjoy the wild places without the traffic of people.

People who plan for such trips are glad for a respite from the modern era. They accept, on nature's terms, its conditions. They know that while it stalks them, they are free to roam and to catch the vibrancy of the land before it sleeps.

TWO

REACHING FOR THE LIGHT

On occasion of every accident (event) that befalls you,
remember to turn to yourself and inquire what power
you have for turning it to use.
Epictetus

So intractable is our will to live that we will do almost anything to have it. That is a lesson nature has taught me.

I see it in so many places, trees that will grow almost horizontal to receive the gift of sunshine — so essential to their well-being and growth. Branches emerge from a cluster of thick pine needles that decide, for some reason, they must not be swallowed by the shadows but must grow into the light.

I see it in small seedlings, no more than a thimble, which compete with brush and ground cover to grandly proclaim they have a place in the emerging landscape. This is discovered, not in summer's heat with its proliferation of life, but in autumn when such plants are revealed.

They grow on the side of roads where they have no reason to propagate. Soon, it is precarious whether snowplows will reach their broad blades out to destroy them.

They grow near great spruce and at the base of birch and aspen trees. They grow among the grasses and sedges, and in the silent places of swamps and muskeg. Here, tamarack seedlings grow.

It seems unlikely they will survive. The odds are so much against them. They are overshadowed by a thicket of stem and weed. Willow prevents them from catching even a small measure of sunlight. Competing trees grow directly next to them. Shadows are cast by a canopy of leaves and branches.

Nevertheless, it is this time of year that one can witness their persistence. Nature is prolific in its willingness to risk, to take advantage of any opportunity, with seed and habitat coming together to create at least this one chance.

Many do not survive. Seeds fall between the crevices, but on the shelf rock of Lake Superior, one is amazed at the wildflowers that seek out the soil in any break between the fissures.

Heading into the Thunder Bay country, one can see high promontories where, from their stone shelves, large trees grow, refusing the stubborn pull of gravity. Theirs is a marginal existence, but they hold on. The sun and roots, like grappling hooks, fix them to the face of the cliff.

I think of this when it comes to adversity in life and how things can be set against us. In many cases, we live in the shadows, or among the rocks. We do not *choose* to live there, but it is where we have been planted.

Perhaps we have been cast into a place where there is little possibility. The canopy of disadvantage or the grasses of lost opportunity seek to crowd us out from true living.

It might be that we only have a rock face to cling to, a small outcropping that splays itself against the sun. We may find ourselves in deep summer, buried in weed or underbrush, where others cannot assess properly whether we are growing, or whether we exist at all.

We may be competing for moisture with our past, with an everyday affliction, with others whose despondent spirits are bringing us down.

It is only in the autumn when we see, in the remnants of the summer, a testament to life's tenaciousness.

As we walk among the fallen leaves, we see nature's ability to use any advantage to promote its growth.

In the spring, before the rising tide of the emergent forest-cover takes over, we can see those survivors of winter that have borne harsh conditions. In the months leading up to the hard frost, it is as though nature relaxes and we can see fledgling places once obstructed by ground cover. One asks: "How could these seedlings make it with no sun and such crowded conditions?" Still, here they are.

Trees damaged by rude storms or embankments that fall

away and expose the root structure, or winds that drive a tree downward, these are all part of a natural cycle. Why one tree falls and another remains standing against erosion or nature's fury can be a mystery to us. There are reasons, but who can predict which tree will break against the storm?

For some, the damage is too great, but I am heartened by the stubborn refusal of other trees to give up their place in life.

To the South, I know of one oak where shoots grow from the horizontal parent limb. These slender branches would not accept their diminished stature.

Eventually, the branch will break from the weight of the log compounded by these offshoots that are growing taller each year. In the meantime, perhaps for the next decade or so, these progeny will dance in the sun.

IN THESE GREY DAYS, we do not have the advantage of the long reach of time to know which colonizers of the new forest will make it.

We do know some will refuse to accept the limitations placed on their young existence. They wait patiently for some sliver of warmth and light.

They grow in places where it is unlikely. They reach (sometimes to their disadvantage) when they are confined to the dark spaces.

THREE

SHOULDER SEASON

A maverick is one who does not fit into the commonplace as others do, nor fall into the expected mold: a stray animal that doesn't want to run with the herd.

Of Time and Place
Sigurd Olson

The end of October, early November, is shoulder season in Minnesota. In spring it happens when the cross-country ski trails are soft and can no longer be used. It is too soon for the fishing season to open. In fall, it comes before the snow and skiers and black diamonds.

Ice has not formed yet out on the lakes. Light is diminishing now. Leaves are on the ground. It is a time of waiting and appreciation.

The long days of summer are but a memory, and there is

a cold pitch to the wind. The sky is different. Long shadows extend out onto the roads while driving. Now we are more conscious of the sun without its warmth and nightfall is coming sooner.

But there are good things during this time as well. Starfields are crystal without the haze of summer humidity. The air is sharp and for breathing. It is a season of purposeful activities, knowing the time is short. Rain keeps us inside close to the fire.

Isn't life like this? Sometimes we enjoy the long days of summer when things are bountiful, and flowers grow along the roadways. But in shoulder seasons we are aware of a shift. It is a time of tending to necessities. It is a time for gathering in, a time for meditation, a time for memories garnered like blueberries from the summer past.

In my work as a marriage therapist, I routinely saw people heading into shoulder season. The flourish of summer seems only remembered. The glow of fading light in the West comes sooner now than it once did. Activities once enjoyed are diminished. Waves picking up along the shore are reminders our relationship, too, is unsettled.

Here are some ideas that can help individuals and couples during such a time.

Shoulder seasons can have negatives, but there are also good things to be reminded of. Yes, life is shutting down (or so it seems). But there is also the promise of life that is different but worthwhile. We can enjoy the time for what we have been given. We shouldn't waste it.

There is much to be done. Winter lies ahead, but it should give us a sense of urgency. We don't want to be performing the usual activities in the snow. We must complete them sooner if possible.

For couples, that means we should intentionally deal with and address problems. We should get the help we need. Otherwise, we pay the price when the winds and frigid cold of December come too early.

The land is devoid of the blazing maple leaves of autumn, but we shouldn't be surprised by this. It is part of a natural cycle.

As we struggle with moods or feelings which are downcast, we should remember that even nature cannot sustain the frenzy of growth.

It must rest. For a time it lies dormant, only to begin again with the turning of the seasons.

The good people who come from the city to see the leaves golden are gone now. And sometimes we, who stay in the border country, must deal with life, more alone. The luxury of mixing with the tourist crowd is no longer possible. People retreat, but that can be a good thing, as we are left to brew cups of hot tea, think longer more deliberate thoughts, learn to live more with ourselves and to brace for the coming winter.

However, while fewer people might greet us, those who we know seem more visible. We cross paths more often. We are more familiar with each other. We can slow down to talk and to catch up before we are caught in more activities.

Autumn can be harsh. We know that. It can seem long. We don't deceive ourselves about this. But we also know spring will come.

Marriages sometimes need to be reminded that problems won't get settled in a day. There is nothing magical that will help us when temperatures hover at 20 below. But that doesn't mean we are without aid and comfort.

We can enjoy other activities alone or together. Yes, we can even choose to get out in the cold with walks, snowshoeing, skiing, fires built upon bases of snow. We can live with the expectation that the Northern Lights, while hidden today by thick cloud cover, might be there tomorrow.

Individuals can also do what is necessary to prepare and "make the best of it" knowing that spring will follow as sure as the sunrise.

IN THIS PART of the world, grain ships make their way up the darkened coast to Thunder Bay. There is a rush to ship cargo before freeze-up. I see their lights, sometimes like small moving cities, glazed upon the horizon. I'm sure they watch for wind warnings. They are all too mindful of the season. The rolling waves remind them life is changing.

They see it as a time of opportunity, while they are also mindful of the things they must do. It is a time of measured caution and opportunity.

Whether you are in a marriage that has a shoulder season, or if you are an individual who can relate to the presence of shoulder seasons in your life, I encourage you to embrace these changes and draw from their lessons.

Time moves and so should you. Find help. Do what you must. Settle in knowing winter is a reality but that the warmth of spring is sure to follow. You may feel alone, but yes, you can also "make the best of it." You can hunker down near a good warm fire.

While devoid of leaves, the land is always good. It is as it should be. It is a normal part of the changing seasons.

FOUR

HYPOTHERMIA: NATURE'S WARNING

Couples think by huddling with knees drawn up to their chests they can save themselves—but sometimes the warmth they have is not enough.

Compass Readings
J Bragstad

Hypothermia is a feature of the North. It can be insidious. I remember reading about a sudden drop in temperature and drizzle that one historic year killed many duck hunters in their blinds and boats.

It is a soft danger. It creeps in without any direct warning. It is easy to minimize the inherent problems that are developing, that soon will turn from discomfort into great peril and difficulty.

I have directly contended with hypothermia three times in my life.

The first was on Otter Lake in northern Saskatchewan. Fishing the islands, my son and I didn't notice the slight drizzle that had begun to fall. We didn't notice how our sweatshirts were becoming damp. Without baseball caps, our hair was becoming wet with the rain. Then the wind tossed up and we quite reasonably made for shore to get out of our sodden clothes.

By the time we arrived, hypothermia had greeted us.

A funny thing happens when the blood leaves the brain to protect our core and vital organs. We begin to lose our ability to concentrate. We become immobile. We tremble noticeably. A person becomes disengaged.

We needed to act, and thankfully we did. But what to do next? Build a fire? Pitch a tent? Get out of our wet clothing? But strangely, once the body has passed a certain threshold, it cannot warm itself. Blankets or sleeping bags are not enough. What to do then? Warm soup might be preferable, but put any of these things in the wrong order, and they will not be sufficient.

The first thing we did was put on stocking caps to stop the river of warmth coming off our heads, where a field of small blood vessels was draining the heat away. The second thing we had to stop was the deleterious effects of the wind, removing heat from our bodies. We put on windbreakers and, with difficulty, pitched our tent as another provision against exposure.

The wet clothes were not our friend, and counterintuitively, we knew we had to remove them to regain warmth. Huddled in a sleeping bag, we relied on each other for body heat, and eventually, conversation returned. There was laughter with relief. At a certain point, we were ready to build a fire.

THERE WERE other times like this. Once a party became too spread out, and I watched two canoeists capsize off a rocky ledge in a windstorm. I came upon them both, dazed, not knowing what to do, standing with arms crossed tightly in front of them. Their misery told me this is how they thought they could keep themselves warm.

They didn't know that over time this would be fatal. It was critical they move and do things such as we had done on Otter to survive. Again, it was counterintuitive. They balked, but for me, there was no choice. It was either this, or they would quickly slip into the seductive graces of hypothermia.

The third time it was ironic. I was with two avid hunters, both men who were experienced in the out-of-doors. The day was beautiful as we left the harbor to move to the far side of the lake to fish. But a curtain of black clouds was being pulled, like a quilt, coming in from the West. We didn't see it until it broke over the trees, and we did the thing that made the most sense. We headed for shore.

Our mistake was in thinking it was a passing shower. We didn't want to bother taking the motor off the canoe. The Grumman could have been used, like a tarp, to shelter us from the rain. Instead, we crouched under the branches of a thicket of small trees. Eventually, the rain overwhelmed this meager protection, drop by drop.

And soon the laughter and stories we were telling were silenced. We drew increasingly into ourselves. With time, three experienced outdoorsmen were sitting on a log fighting our individual battles, with the deep trembling and chills coming from inside.

In desperation, we finally broke, took a big chance, got back into our canoe and crossed the lake, very much aware of the lightening in an aluminum canoe. It was dangerous and, on any other occasion, it would have been reckless. But we had done the math and knew this was calculated to be our only chance. Hypothermia could not be ignored.

In my work as a marriage counselor, I often saw this same dynamic: people who are overcome by patterns that, like gentle rain, eventually get into the quality and health of their relationship.

The winds of day-to-day interactions and memories of hurtful events continue to blow. Couples become immobile.

They think that by standing and protecting themselves, or huddled with knees drawn up to their chests, that they can save themselves.

But sometimes the warmth we have is not enough. We have crossed the threshold.

We need another's encouragement, support, caring, acceptance and understanding, their willingness to try to be present with us to survive relationally. Seldom do we experience this.

Couples in my practice almost always wanted to start with the problems. But this is akin to building a fire without dry clothes, without the safety of a windbreak, with internal body temperatures plummeting.

There is a time for matches and hot soup, a time for naming and discussing real problems. Someday we might want to think about how we got to the situation we find ourselves in. But now, this is a faulty prioritization. There is not enough warmth in the relationship. There is not enough safety, where things can be talked about with some perspective and distance from the immediate problem.

Increasingly in my work, I began sessions by talking about what has been positive in the last week? What has each person noticed in the other person's behavior that has been meaningful to them? What have they appreciated — in going the extra mile? What has made a *real* difference, even if it is only a slight one?

That is not easy to do in some cases. We are so bent in on our misery. But otherwise, if we fail to do this, the other person who has tried may feel their efforts are of no value. They are going it alone. There is no reinforcement. And we think the same way if our best moments are not recognized.

Sharing affirmatively like this is a form of huddling together. Ever so slowly, things begin to shift.

It is not everything but, strategically, it is something. The one thing we might need to do in these circumstances.

Individuals face this same problem as the steady effects of life trickle down on them. Soon they are cold and trembling.

It is not easy to think about what to do when they are concerned only for their well-being at the most basic level.

What can one do to warm oneself?

Well, probably what you are doing (if things are not improving) should be discontinued. What might be counter-intuitive to your own experience? In what order should things be done? That can make a real difference.

Is what I'm doing "enough" when I think about what will happen over time if I don't do everything I need to do to regain warmth and equilibrium.

THESE ARE all hard questions to consider when we are exposed to rough conditions, to sudden changes, to the unwavering winds of life. Hypothermia steals in upon us, and we cannot underestimate what it will do to us if left unattended.

Of course, we often don't have the will to do what we must. Our thinking might be confused. However, we must rouse ourselves to do what is necessary. Otherwise, it may be a form of standing out on the rocks with the unrelenting wind stripping our bodies of warmth.

Counseling, something we might never have considered, may be of the highest priority now. Like slipping out of our wet clothes, we may not want to do it. But is it necessary? Do conditions warrant it? Or can we wait? And for how long?

It is all a question of judgment and timing. Paying attention to what our situation demands. Having a healthy respect for when is the optimum time to reach decisions — and when we just might wait too long.

At some point laughter returns. Things get discussed. People move out of survival mode.

The rains might continue, and the breezes will most certainly sweep over the lake, but circumstances have changed. People find themselves back in control. They rest easy, safe and warm, the two basics of life.

That is the time when meaningful conversation can take place, when it is time to once again plot your course.

FIVE

WOODSHED

Let my warmth and glow caress you,
for your trails are grim and hard;
Let my arms of comfort press you,
hunger-hewn and battle-scarred:

Oh, my lovers! How I bless you with
your lives so madly marred.

The Song of the Camp-Fire
Robert Service

With the approach of the deep snow woodsheds that are stacked bring real comfort. There is more work to be done but knowing that provision has been made for heat can be a great satisfaction to anyone living here. It is its own measure of wealth.

I have had winters where supplies of birch and oak,

aspen, and pine run low. Instead of bounty one must calculate carefully whether need will outstrip supply. Occasionally, a person must return to the woods to hunt under snowdrifts for anything left, as an afterthought, when winter flurries are in the air. Then, labor is cumbersome, and cold penetrates. We know all too well the maxim: "When you cut wood you are warmed twice."

In this regard, we do not live well on credit. Allowing ourselves the luxury of knowing things can be had later is not a way to calm winter nights. Sitting in front of the fire, watching its coals dwindle down, is it not a great thing to know life, at this level, has been provided for?

We are used to the promise of furnaces, knowing that propane dealers can deliver at almost any time when roads allow. But when they can't get out, when we are destitute of ordinary, everyday elements such as heat, are we not reminded of how fragile and precarious our living conditions might be?

When we are interconnected and reliant on others in almost every station of life, have we lost the realization we must make it occasionally on our own?

Self-reliance is the wood's message. It is a reminder I am not invulnerable.

I remember days when we put these logs away. I remember the anticipation of how comfortable this seasoned wood will keep us. I am connected to a time when things may go badly and, I believe, even if I am isolated, I can still prevail.

Do we live like this anymore in any respect? People who invest are dependent upon the vicissitudes of the stock market that can give as well as take. As a culture, we have become dependent on rains that do not come for our fruits and some vegetables. We are dependent on the electronics in our cars.

A grid goes down, and computers store so much of our lives. Our children live out of calculators and, in some cases, are confused when asked to give out change in a manner other than what the cash register tells them.

It is an enriching society but a more fragile one. Through a whole series of incremental inventions and changes, we have discovered a world our grandparents could have only imagined back in the 1900s. I'm sure that was true for their parents as well. Leading into the future, it will astound others as they measure our lifestyle by what is about to take place.

Woodsheds are humble dwellings. Other than the wind penetrating and an occasional mouse, they are nothing spectacular when compared to terabytes of data or the ability to transport oneself to Paris in a matter of hours.

Woodsheds, for much of the year, are not needed and rarely do we go there. They are an afterthought. They provide little to our lives.

But in winter, as the cold approaches, they take on greater importance. These denizens of the forest have served us well in keeping dry and secure the things that matter most. It is a hardship when cabins burn down. It can also be life-threatening when wood is not to be found in places where frozen conditions are on the move, pressing down on the land's inhabitants. Then, woodsheds hold one of life's great treasures.

Wood is known for its quality. Aspen is no less precious but burning comes quickly and not a lot of heat is thrown off. Pine sends sparks and, while it is scented, does not burn long either.

Tamaracks, grown in ancient swamps, are like tinder, hot and then turned to ashes. Oak is that rare find, as well as a good birch, that can carry conversations well into the night before fires are restocked.

Propane gives few memories, but I have a treasure of recollections from gathering wood, bringing it home, and stacking it up for the winter.

In the Red River country of Manitoba, there is not a lot of wood to be discovered. It grows mostly along rivers that cut through the vast expanses of flat prairie. I remember a time when friends would invite me to cut fallen trees with them. Great pieces of oak that had gone down the previous winter were there in the gullies and low places. We would section them into pieces and throw them into the back of the truck.

To this day I still see their pristine character, hard and dry, and their size which dwarfs perhaps a half-a-century. To cut them into thick slats to later fit into our wood stove was extravagant in that country, as was the banter and company of those good men now gone from my life.

In Saskatchewan, the sweet smell of aspen charged the fall days with an aroma one can never forget. There, forests were offered by farmers as a gift for me, to harvest selectively. They would show me how to cut the wood, how to contend with the falling of a tree. We would load up and take these logs back to town.

They would remind us all that season, whenever we would go to fetch more for the fire, of those gracious days in dank, sweet-smelling forests.

Woodsheds are something in life there are not enough of.

Where are these places for you where you have stored up a different kind of wealth? Are they in your grandchildren? Your memories of great vacations or in your past, where once life was more elemental but seemed to be worth more?

WHAT IS THERE that is concrete in your life that can be measured not just by potential, but by real substance? What is it that occasionally the wind blows through, where perhaps a mouse might reside, that stands as a hedge against winter's cold?

What will warm you in days to come?

How intentional have you been in putting other things aside, to spend time on what, in the end, will be the thing that matters?

Soon the December moon will rise over stretches of country that are home to the moose, deer, beaver, and wolf. Soon lakes will crack under the burden of an increasingly oppressive cold. It is the nature of the North.

Will I be ready to meet its demands that are harsh, yes, but common to the natural occurrence of things?

SIX

DAYS OF BRAZEN COLOR

*I am glad I shall never be young
without wild country to be young in.*

*Of what avail are forty freedoms
without a blank spot on the map?*

A Sand County Almanac
Aldo Leopold

The day was delirious. Fall colors from red maple, golden aspen, mixed with the muted greens of the pine. It was a day of splendor, driving the abbreviated backroads among the hills. Later the breezes would toss the leaves and scatter them, but today it was all perfect.

Sometimes life can be that frenetic, too alive with splendid colors that don't quite match our experience. It is more than "enough." It is electric. Gazing up into the sun-swelled trees, such experiences dwarf the routine days that draw summer on.

Then, days are beautiful but not like this. With that first tinge of frost in the air, things come out of solstice to peak in the coveys and along the crest of the hills.

I have been told it is not entirely certain why leaves lose the chlorophyll that fills them. Some say it is the length of days. Others claim it is the cold that affects delicate root structures and the spawn of vital energies to the rest of the tree.

What is most interesting is that the blaze of colors we see are the tree's *true* colors. Summer masks this and hides it. But with the approach of winter, conditions allow the branches and leaves to reveal themselves.

In retirement, I think about transformation while walking the paths and portages and open spaces of the canoe country.

> Here, in this explosion of red and yellow and auburn and scarlet and vermillion, there is no self-deprecation. As the days darken, it is as though the trees take one last great swing for the fences.

They become truly what they are. While their time is brief, it is well-lived, and they go out holding nothing back.

It is a time of greater silence, of shadows lengthening, of good days and sudden shifts in the weather. But, it is as though nature itself knows it is its time to celebrate the growth of summer and to shed the leaves that hold the snow and ice of coming winter.

It occurs to me retirement mimics these days of quiet activity. Even the fish are coming into the shallows now. The stars are brighter, but we stay out less.

Fires warm us, but we must have made provision for them storing up wood that is not green or full of moisture.

Suddenly daylight seems so much shorter. We are thinking it might be our last fishing trip for this year and are measuring when it is time to clean the wood stove chimney.

Here, we have the opportunity to become the person we are. Periods of productivity give way, as the shortness of the day, or a lapse in physical energy, reminds us time is becoming short. It is a time when we shouldn't hold back.

It is a time when we must venture into the heart of the country, leave the familiar lakes along the shore to spend more time in places that will soon be buried in snowdrifts.

LATER WILL BE the time for the tamarack growing in the swamps and sedges to glow with the warm yellows of autumn. It is another of my favorite times when branches have been stripped and stand like sketches against the sky.

By this point, there will likely be frost gathering on the grasses in the land of the beaver and occasional moose. Tamaracks are a hearty tree that grows slowly. They too will mark the changing of the season.

Perhaps both will be offered to me, the time to show forth what has been delayed through years of activity and raising a family. A second moment after life has lost much of its wild energy, when I can still enjoy the more somber aspects of the season in places more secluded and primal.

It is interesting to me, that even on days when trees are bereft of their leaves, undiscovered lakes can be seen where once they were hidden.

SEVEN

SUPERIOR: FIRST LIGHT

The dwarf whirled round but it was already too late. "The sun's rays arrest you," gloated Thor, "and they turn you into stone. And now the sun shines in my hall once again."

The Norse Myths
Kevin Crossley-Holland

Dawn is the perfect marriage between the light glowing in the southerly sky and the pale reflection set out on the lake. Living near Lake Superior, there are the broad expanses that one does not have living in the woods or along the streets of our larger cities.

I have talked particularly to people from England who live on the prairie, where stark and flat fields extend off to capture the horizon. Many have told me they don't mind these large spaces where, as one poet, Wallace Stegner, has put it: "This is a land to mark the sparrow's fall." The reason, they say, is because it is very much reminiscent of Britain. Living close to the ocean, it has the same character and form.

As I watch the wheat stems waving and giving substance to the wind, detecting its every nuance and motion, I can see how they might feel at home in places like southern Manitoba and Saskatchewan. Here are the vast and broad spaces, the great sphere of light where nothing obstructs one's view.

Here there are no secrets. The sun coming up either rises (as the Canadian songwriter Stephen Fearing says) as an "arc-weld" or it hesitates and presses through dark bands of clouds or smudges that later on will seem an afterthought.

Waves on Superior also tell a part of the story. Sometimes they are mountainous. Sometimes they minuet off in different directions responding to some strange quirk of nature that seems undecided. Against the fading darkness, they contrast to a sky that is often passive and calm. They support the passage of ships this time of year and the occasional presence of ducks that speckle in small numbers of three or four.

One woman I knew well, who visited us in both environments, the lake and the fields of Saskatchewan, would describe how it is for her to see this ancient dance of the rising sun. At her home, it was always obstructed by houses. By the time she would catch first light, the sun had already tempered its shape and color. No more were there embers lying cast about on the horizon-line, coals waiting for fire.

Unaccustomed to this, it was a great privilege for her to

witness such a common sight along the North Shore or on the prairies.

This time of year daylight has shifted quite dramatically to the South from out of the East. The constellation Orion is just beginning to rise. The long line of golden diamond reflection of the new day on the water allows, for moments, the eye's passage to see its full splendor.

Hours later the sun will become white gold that distracts and distresses anyone looking out over the lake. It can be harmful to sight to stare at it, but now, in the early morning, it is a pathway broken only by the waves glittering and in motion.

We see the sun rising, but the truth is it is we who are moving. As the earth rotates, it is spinning at the equator at approximately one thousand miles per hour. Sometimes we have to be reminded that we, who seem so stable, are the ones who are being flung through the galaxy.

In a world often encompassed by ego, it is easy to think of ourselves as primary at the beginning of each new day.

It is easy to think the sun rises and sets with us. Blocked from seeing this miracle because of intellect, or a busy mind, or a technology that gives us the tools to dictate much of nature's raw dimension, we view the sun with very little distinction in its shape and color. It passes through the sky relatively unnoticed until the gleam of sunset removes it from us.

Dawn marks a different kind of moment in each day's history as does the eventide. Here the world is alive not only with possibility, but it also takes on new relevance. Instead of the bland rising through the day, the sun is from another world where we both cast off darkness and welcome its arrival. For moments, the world suspends and takes notice.

People who have waited out the night and the deep darkness of early morning anticipate with suspense, knowing already the ending of this mystery.

Similarly, it is the setting sun that might cause us to reflect, to tally up our day. It might ask of us what we did that was of substance? It measures, in ways calendars often do not, the passing of our days. As it draws to an end, we can experience its peace. It marks finally a moment when we can catch our breath.

NATURE PUTS us in touch with this unfolding more than being in the city. Those driving to work might note in passing the indirect reflection of dawn on skyscraper build-ings, but they see little else. Their minds are already preoc-cupied with the news or tasks they must complete before the end of the day. It is a race with the sun as much as it is with the clock to get everything accomplished.

But next to Lake Superior, looking out towards Batchawana Bay in eastern Ontario, there is less to distract, more to see and more reason to slow down to observe and take it in.

Such small acts connect us with the world we are a part of. Who can watch the sunrise and not stop to enjoy this precious minute of time and pay tribute to it? The rest of the day might be onrushing, but here the world will wait while another drama that is not scripted by our devices, plays out.

Only then is it time to begin our work.

EIGHT

FOREST UNDERCOVER

For now, we see in a mirror, dimly, but then
face to face. Now I know in part, but then
I shall know just as I also am known.

1 Corinthians 13:6
St. Paul of Tarsus

I t's interesting how the forest strips itself away before winter. Leaves are gone now. They lie scattered on the ground, far from the blush of warm summer days when they would challenge the sun. Skies are often leaden, and soon the gales of November will be upon us.

It is a time of quiet punctuated by the odd hunter who has discovered a grouse along some forest path or in a clearing. Some would say it is a time of melancholy, a time of brooding.

It is a restless time, in some respects, as we wait for the

first sign of snow. Temperatures are dropping and nights are not confident they will hold the frost. Woodsmoke is in the air in unexpected places. It is a time of gathering. It is also a time that invites reflection.

Soon the skiers will be pirouetting down the ridges and fall-lines. Cross-country skiers will remember tracks not taken all summer and will herringbone their way up sloping hills, taking them to vistas and promontories overlooking the canoe country.

It is a time when wolves and deer run freely before the deep drifts of winter snows. A time for deer to test themselves in the rut. A time when trout begin to move in from the deep waters of the lake.

It is also time when the ore boats come closer to the rocks on the margins of the great sea known as Superior. A time when gardens are spent, when wild berries are rare and ever more precious. It is a time of eagles that catch every movement from their perch on some deadfall-burdened tree.

The forest cover that once was so prolific is now gone. It has withered over weeks, but seemingly in a day or two, it is down. The land lies open.

Small seedlings are now evident. Each one occasions a surprise of delight. We know they have survived the clutch of summer with its dense growth.

Logs that have been dropped are less hidden by the underbrush. Perhaps there is still time to turn them into fire for my wood-stove if snows will hold off.

Forest undercover is so much of our lives. There is so much hidden by the tangle of rose bushes, broad-leafed aster, willow and yes, even thistle and the non-native species like yellow tansy and lupine.

In the summer, such plants can make any underlying discoveries impenetrable.

I had looked for pine seedlings planted the year before during those summer months and had given up, fearing that to find one I might step on others.

People complain about how much 'stuff' they have. Perhaps it is not the excess (even the forest fills in and is opportunistic in utilizing empty spaces) but what is hidden that intuitively they know they will never see. Days of autumn allow us to see more clearly what is left, what is growing, the things that did not make it.

Age is perhaps an autumnal paring down of experiences.

We might long for springtime with all its fever and new life. We might look back on summer with its intense storing up and production. But the fall gives us deeper insight even as branches divest themselves of leaves.

It is a good thing we have to wait for winter. In the land's eternal wisdom, this rhythm allows us time to pause and to make ready.

The ice will come soon enough, but for now, plants have time to replenish and draw back vital energies they will need to protect themselves while waiting for the spring.

How much are we like them? In the rhythms of our lives, when the joy of extravagance is transmuted to harvest time, when the undergrowth suddenly is spent and leaves drift down day-by-day from the trees and swirl along country roads, to know we are given time to examine where growth has taken root. To search for where life is emerging and where there is more still to do.

This is not only true of old age, where it is even more evident. It is true also for the young, where adulthood comes upon them sometimes too quickly, and they need time to reflect and gather up from their experiences. It is true for those who separate in relationships, who must discover meaning in what was lost.

Dreams altered or abandoned can hold the promise of something new. There, in the underbrush and tangle of life, discoveries can be made that a person may not have been aware of before.

How often do we spend time wishing for the sun when the undertones of autumn will do? Winter comes soon enough but, still, even now, there is so much to see.

NINE

RIVERS RUN DRY

*The secular school attempts to explain things
and creates knowledge. The religious school
teaches one to contemplate things in such
a way that it creates wonder.*

Mastering Sadhana
Carlos G. Valles, S.J.

I n the spring there is the wild ecstasy of water cascading down the sides of the hills towards Lake Superior. It forms rivulets that gather into canyons of rock that over centuries have carved out paths to this ancient sea.

Rivers this time of year do not look like that. For the most part, they are dry as fall reaches into the winter months. They will have their purpose later when snow-melt gathers in the high country, but now they are merely tributes to the birth of spring. Such riverbeds are mute. There is no song to be sung.

I think of this as a testament to so much of life. Rivers run dry. As a writer, I am aware of this. Some days it is as though the waters themselves were writing my words. They rush to me faster than I can write them down.

Other days are not like this. Writing does not come easy. There is nothing to say. There is no inner impulse to offer something tangible either to myself or others. The creek is dry, and the rocky ravines leading to the lake are empty.

Perhaps that is true for you as well. Perhaps that is life. We take in information and stimuli and we enjoy moments when there is a confluence, where it all comes together, and we ride its rising tide to the limit.

But then, it is gone. It drains away. Ideas do not stop, but they recede.

When do rivers stop running here? It is hard to say but, one day the currents are gone. Imposing cliffs that once spilled over with water are now rock faces that follow me as I walk along the highway.

Relationships can also be like this. Spring will come. But in the days when an autumn sky is cast in leaden gray, rains can be sparse here in Minnesota.

The life-force seems to be missing. There is no snowmelt. There is no excess, as water levels have gone down over the summer. Then, we remember what it was like when canyons flowed with currents, playfully, joyfully, frolicking with ease down the hillsides.

We might recall how easy it was to explore a river's upper reaches, to have moments of sitting beside them or walking in their waters. Then, the land was being warmed and we were enjoying the great bounty of May, June, and July.

How hard it is now to think we may have nothing to give, that waters have receded. There are days we are reminded that what was once so much a part of the joy of our experience is now but a relic written in stone.

We observe the cut-faces and potholes and craggy pitches where water has left evidence of its passing, but now there is little magic in such static places as these.

Living in a land where winter will soon impose its own story, we must remember that, even as it does so, it is writing a new chapter in the snows that accumulate deep in the shadows, between the lakes and on the lake surfaces.

In the frozen places there is the precursor of spring's run-off. It may not seem apparent, but the land is patient and will wait.

I go to the border to witness the ageless display of spring as the waters of the Pigeon River, ancient highway of the native and voyageur, spill over and drop some 120 feet. It is a remarkable event to be there when, in a great gathering, eager waters organize in their race to Superior.

But then, I also go in autumn to a bridge where I stand and search for trickles of water moving under the hard-scrabble of flat rocks leading to the lake. It is quite an ordinary site, but different from times when I know it will be more than a dried-up creek bed.

Even then, I am grateful for what it holds as it waits patiently for another day.

TEN

CHIK-WAUK

*For me, the River of No Return has become a symbol of life.
Yesterday is always gone forever, a part of the river we have
already run. Tomorrow is always unknown, a part of the river
that lies ahead, around a bend, hidden by the towering walls
of the canyon.*

By the River of No Return
Don Ian Smith

I n Ojibwe, Chik-Wauk means "Jack of the Pines," a strange reference of what origin I am not sure. It hides from me in internet searches.

As I walked the path leading from the museum at the end of the incomparable Gunflint Trail, I became aware of another reality that traces itself through time and place.

Chik-Wauk is a stone-faced reminder of the past nestled just outside the Boundary Waters Canoe Area. From a graceful backwater pond, it releases to a channel taking you to Saganaga, one of the most beautiful lakes author Sigurd Olson said he had ever known in his wilderness travels.

Skirting the quiet shores, following past an old relic dock being reclaimed by the land, the trail brushes by a spur that leads to an overlook. Here we could look down from where we had departed.

Except for the red roof of the nature center and a few automobiles parked in the adjacent driveway, the scene was timeless. Great rocks spun out of the water. The fires that had passed through this region were not on that side of the bay. White pine and strong black spruce watched over Chik-Wauk, and it was itself but a small indentation on the wild places surrounding us.

Those who had reconstructed the resort's main lodge and had made it a museum and nature center had placed something here, not often found in the canoe country. Here, the emphasis has been on returning the land to what it had been.

There is a single photo mounted on a metal stand, like an extended hand pointing back to the museum building. I could see this scene as it is now but also, in that picture, I could see what it was then.

As I put landmarks together, I could glimpse empty strands of reeds and grasses now, juxtaposed with sandy beaches next to sculpted channels, from that time past.

I saw a Forest Service Jon boat tied to a single wooden pier. I noticed that once there had been at least three boat docks. There was melancholy for days gone by.

So much life and elegance lost with the coming of the Wilderness Act. The red roofs on the photograph were the same as the museum but instead of a single building now, then there were neat structures on shore filled with oars and outboard motors. They graced a long pier leading to a timbered boathouse nesting but a single wooden launch. It was as elegant for the North as anything you might have seen in some of the gentle lakes of central Wisconsin.

I counted almost thirty boats from that picture, either lining the beach or out in the bay. Canoes were present, a single canoe with a couple in the bay paddling out for perhaps a day's excursion. Motorboats in this shallow, obscure place were waiting to dock.

It was a moment I don't think I will ever forget. It was a postcard found from long ago.

That photo transported me to a simpler, romantic time when there was less travel, less speed, less satiation, less of everything.

A caption underneath the picture put it succinctly: what I was witnessing was "The heyday of resorts in a fisherman's paradise at the end of the Gunflint Trail."

I'm sure many will be glad that these artifacts have been removed, and albeit for this picture, have been forgotten. All the buildings except for the lodge were burned after falling into disrepair. The beach regressed to what it had been before the coming of the resort. Gone were the open, graceful landing spaces. Sedges and wild grasses had now encroached upon this shore and had taken over.

Sigurd Olson was right. Wilderness is an intangible perhaps made more apparent by what is not seen. There are no "improvements" here.

My son writes to tell me in the whirl of his business obligations that reading Olson's books are a counter-balance to the frenetic world he lives in. He speaks not so much of the reminiscences of trips into the canoe country but of eternal values. For Olson, it is the spiritual that underscores and is nurtured by such a close acquaintance with the land itself.

This, more than setting aside recreational land and preserving it from timber and mining companies, was what Olson and many others were fighting for.

On that day I was reminded that others were compelled to give up the life they had known with the establishment of the Wilderness Act in 1964. They were required to leave, or the government bought them out.

We experience a new way of life when we take to the trails but, for them, this was not an excursion up from Minneapolis to enjoy fresh breezes and long, lingering glances at waves as they marched in towards the shore. For many, this had become their home, and places like those in that picture were not just a forgotten postcard. It was their life.

At a camp I worked at just this side of the Canadian border, many of the camp's buildings were dismantled, cabins taken down and removed from what would become the BWCA. Those places are gone now, as are the cabins that died in the fires of the 1950s and 60's. But someone built them. Someone inhabited the land. Someone perhaps was making a good life for their family.

In our longing for true wilderness, we can forget it doesn't only comprise nature and the inhabitants that winter there, in dens or those that fly in from the South in springtime. Once people were living here, in what are now "designated conservation" lands. They knew the joy of putting a sill log in place as they joined in what for them was the preeminent adventure, even if born of necessity.

Before this, aboriginal people were here. Pictographs tell their story.

I THINK OF WHAT WAS "ENTERTAINMENT" for the people in that photo, who brought activity to what was then not called the Boundary Waters? I think of those now who immerse themselves in a different kind of entertainment, in electronics and summer skill camps. Enjoyment and preoccupation with these, along with changing demographics, might signal the eventual return of the land to "emptiness."

Of course, the bear, the eagle, the raven will be there. The quiet will be known by the otter and the great horned owl. The rapids will run, but what will turn the generations back to values wilderness nurtures, such as hard work, self-reliance, an independent spirit, to listening as the wind sweeps quietly over the hills?

I am now retired from the world of work I have found fulfilling. It has been a good journey. But increasingly I find myself looking at the picture of who I was professionally, and I juxtapose it with a very different image of who I am now. Strangely, the landmarks are the same, but who I now appear to be is very different.

So it is with mothers. Their children slip by grade school, and the scene is forever changed. The activities once so meaningful are gone. The shores are now lined with grasses. "Boathouses" that once made everything so festive will be removed as childhood toys are put away for the grandchildren.

This was not an empty time
but a time that has passed.

I expect that's true of many places in our lives that once were vibrant and full and now stand empty. There is joy in the quiet, as there was happiness in the activity of another day.

Perhaps wilderness reflects this, a return to what is more elemental, a slowing down, engaging with life now on its own terms, the removal of distractions. Perhaps wilderness makes us more fit for old age.

This was a haunting place for me, this resting overlook off the trail leading to Blueberry Hill.

Chik-Wauk, the ancient word of the Ojibwe, has (like them) been translated into something new. It is no longer the place for people of another era, who might have thought the festivity there would go on forever.

It is now 'ours.' Someday our way-of-life might be as quaint or removed as theirs. This is my tribute to each one of those intrepid people who, no less than I, found this land a place to enjoy, to wait out its inclement weather, to pick berries in the same way.

It is a tribute to those who laughed, who searched

within, who on moonless nights played cards around the table by kerosene or candlelight at the end of the road.

It is a recognition that they too felt on the edge of adventure inspired by this great place, even with motorboats quietly rocking against the sure boards of the dock, now fallen.

The resorts, built here, and subsequently removed, were places of the North not far from places such as St. Paul, but entirely removed from the ordinariness of everyday life. The people during that time were as much a part of the setting as I when encountering other canoe parties paddling up the shore.

We too are part of this great land and legacy. Our history cannot remove us from that and from its memory.

NORTH: WINTER COLD

What concerns me is that we all live properly in all respects during the winter. Sleep and eat well, so that we have full strength and are in good spirits when spring arrives to fight towards the goal which we must attain at any cost.

Roald Amundson

The Last Place on Earth
Roland Huntford

ONE

THE ENSUING DARKNESS

The Northern Lights have seen queer sights,
But the queerest they ever did see
Was that night on the marge of Lake Laberge
I cremated Sam McGee.

Collected Poems
Robert Service

A s it has been for eons of time, northern-dwellers must learn to cope with the ensuing darkness. It will be like this now for several months, each day progressively shorter. December 21, the solstice, eventually comes, but even here light and dark take a long time to crawl out of their respective positions.

People have adjusted in these latitudes, in caves, birch-bark dwellings, and small cabins on the fringes of civiliza-tion. We also recognize the inherent dangers of being too close for too long a time. Nerves can be on edge, with even the smallest thing, and long periods of night seep into the Vitamin D-deprived aspects of our psyche.

In a recent issue of *Minnesota Conservation Volunteer* magazine, an article appeared with the curious title *"The Necessity of Darkness."*

Do we need darkness? What would happen if we were suddenly plunged into an eternal day? What happens to people close to the equator who cannot see, with the unaided eye, some 2,000 stars shining in the night sky in places far from the glow of city lights?

The author, Peter M. Leschak, asks the question that, given there are 100 billion stars in our universe, "Why is the natural night sky of the Earth so dark?" He adds: "Why doesn't our sky blaze with the hot, white light of innumerable alien suns?"

Have you considered this? He suggests, with an expanding universe, that wavelengths from distant, receding stars change and lose sufficient energy. It makes stars appear to grow dimmer to our eyes.

This "necessity for darkness," could it be that at this night-encircled time of the year, darkness should be revisited and looked at in a different "light"?

I am reminded of a commercial I've seen recently on television where a woman who is blind talks about the enervating effects of a drug that allows her body to "remember" the differences between night and day. Circadian rhythms we take for granted become confused in this netherworld where light is indistinguishable from blackness.

Perhaps, in the course of our lives, we need the absence of light for specified periods. In addition to restfulness, it gives us an opportunity to distance ourselves from the pressing needs of the day, the "hot, white light" of our experience. It allows us a fresh start come morning.

In the circuitous world of the imagination, dreams and sleep rhythms provide us with night vision to reconfigure daily concerns in a different, more meaningful way. Carl Jung, with his emphasis on archetypes and rich symbolic language, gives us a pathway into discerning how dreams make sense of reality — those things we ignore during the fever of wakefulness.

The omnipresence of the night can be overwhelming when daylight cedes around 4:30 p.m. For places to the far north, of course, it is much earlier. In the Yukon and Alaska, darkness can seem eternal as does the day with the coming of the summer solstice.

The poet, Kahlil Gibran, in his efforts to humanize Jesus in his book *Jesus: The Son of Man*, points to the desolation that can be brought on by life lived in darkness.

In his short chapter, he uses this comment by a fictional character to describe Jesus' true nature:

He was impatient with those who weighed and measured the day and the night before they would trust their dreams to dawn or eventide.

Some of us do this. Night is so preponderant that we lose sight of the fact day is coming. Or we fail to see how night might be a gift to us. In the darkness, we overthink and can lose perspective. Long hours are spent deliberating. We have a hard time releasing, letting go. With each dawn (or eventide) there is the possibility of new beginnings.

Abraham Lincoln saw a different value in darkness. Richard Brookhiser, in his book *A Man of Many Faces*, chronicled how Lincoln integrated the wisdom of many male figures into his life and thinking. People like George Washington, Thomas Paine, Thomas Jefferson were among them.

However, during the most painful periods, during the crush of the Civil War as thousands lay dying or dead, Lincoln would reflect on this gathering gloom:

> *If after endeavoring to do my best (to end the war)*
> *I find my efforts fail, I must believe that for some purpose*
> *unknown to me, He wills it otherwise.*

He turns to Mystery. He suggests that in the darkness nothing might be known, but that does not mean it has no purpose. It is just not yet clearly seen or deciphered.

People like St. John of the Cross, a seventeenth-century mystic, knew of this as well. In his classic work, *The Dark Night of the Soul,* he writes:

> *If a (person) wishes to be sure of the road they travel, they*
> *must close their eyes and travel in the dark.*

And again,

> *Faith is a dark night for us, but in this very way gives light.*

With the acceptance of the need for darkness, St. John of the Cross discovered in the impenetrable, things he could not have known or rationally concluded. It was his willingness to enter into the dark without being consumed by it that brought him, in the end, knowledge of the divine.

Darkness is a counterpoint to light. It casts shadows, but it also illuminates by defining the boundaries of things. It gives objects, and ideas, form and substance and character.

There is daylight to follow. However, in the early watches, it seems hard to imagine. Ask anyone who wakes an hour before first light. Here the darkness can be unassailable unless moonlight is cast upon the water.

The coming of the night awakens us to the imperatives of life, what we must do with the limited time we are given.

It is a sort of life coach that is pushing us to take note of time's passing.

Jim Brandenburg is a photographer I deeply admire for his skill, but also for how he transforms pictures into art and magic. At the back of his recent book, he uses one eye-catching phrase to describe a goal he had set for himself. He aimed to take ninety pictures in three months without the luxury of taking more than one photograph in every twenty-four hour period. A single snap of the shutter would send him home.

He wrote:

"Today, I respectfully replay that same dance (of those who

*would scrawl pictographs on the walls of ancient caves)
while being chased only by the light of a swift and
hungry day."*

Those who live in the North appreciate this. The day is moving on. Light is limited. It is hungry to the extent it will devour those who ignore it and those who take full advantage of it. It is for us to decide whether we will be conscious of this fact — and use the time well.

TWO

UNFOUND RICHES

*Yet, compared with a wretched little salmon stream and its
handful of scrawny creeks, these noble rivers meant little. For
in the Klondike Valley, gold lay more thickly than on any
other creek.*

*But white men sought gold along the Yukon for a generation
before they found it.*

Klondike
Pierre Berton

It is winter now and days are short. The rocky ledges
lining Lake Superior are glazed with ice and are dangerous. It is a time of silence when the birds are scarce, and
deer are not moving. There is little snow this year, and frost
runs deep.

Thankfully, the lake is open and sunlight dances across its waves as they move in from the Southwest. It is the month of Long Shadows. The snow is tinged blue in places where balsam fir and pine block the sun from penetrating.

Yesterday I filled our two bird-feeders with sunflower seeds, a staple of the nuthatch, pine siskin, and chickadee, and the occasional squirrel. They have yet to visit. I suppose unfamiliarity means they no longer come here. It has been too long. Where once there was abundance it has been a long time since the feeders were full.

Either they have learned to seek out some other neighbor who has faithfully provided for them or they hunker down in the cold prepared to forage what they can from the forest.

I am impatient. I wait for them. I know, at the first sign, one bird will seemingly tell another.

I think to myself, there will be rejoicing, but not yet. All is prepared, but this source of food is still undiscovered. I wonder how long it will be? I wonder if, for some, it will be too late?

I think about people who are depressed or people whose marriages have fallen on hard times, where winter is all too apparent. I think of those who forage as best they can, unaware of the riches that might be relatively close by.

We don't think to look because experience tells us there is nothing there. We might have gone back to the source a time or two but have come away empty. We may have grown cynical and think it is hopeless to believe life, or our relation-ship could be this good again.

The winter's cold can persuade us to hole up. On days when temperatures dip far below zero, life appears motion-less. Energy is at a premium and cannot be wasted.

If we are overrun with problems, we want to preserve often what we have. We are limited to what we think we know. We hide. We seek the safety of small places, often in shadows, out of the wind.

ON DAYS SUCH AS THIS, even the possibility of unfound riches can seem remote. They can appear beyond our ability to want to seek them out. We don't think to look because experience tells us there is nothing there.

That is what I am afraid of. The birds are used to flying over my little property and for the long month of December they have exhausted whatever seed was available. They might have returned once, maybe again, but then they gave up and looked to other means to survive.

In marriages or relationships, we do the same thing. We do something vital to please our partner, something unchar-acteristic of what has been routine and it isn't received. Our partner doesn't go there. A special meal, a gift, a surprise weekend, a word of endearment are all seemingly undiscov-ered by our partner.

In our personal life our gifts, talents, capabilities, the things people say to us by way of compliment are lost. We have drawn too far inward. It is good food waiting still for discovery.

We retreat into the nooks and crannies of life where we try to survive the cold. Places where we remember joy we don't return to. Experience convinces us these are empty and untended.

MY EXPERIENCE IS THAT OFTEN, as with my bird-feeders, life replenishes itself. Sometimes we need to go back. Sometimes life can surprise us.

I think of that first bird who will come to the feast I have set out for them. How and why this is found, I will never know. I expect it might be by chance. I would like to think these fragile wisps of feather are on the hunt, not satisfied with their place in the willows.

But when one of their kind spots that first seed, it discovers there are more, and the whole community of birds in the area are affected.

It is my experience, as a therapist, that it is not so much insight but reconnecting people with their strengths that provide enough to stem the winter's cold. Here again, these abilities often lie dormant. Successes in one place do not migrate to other areas, areas which desperately need to be shored up and animated by known achievements.

While the winter winds may not have changed, the birds receive what they need to get by, to perhaps make it into the balmy breezes of March and April. I will have had a hand in it. For this, I am grateful. But more than that, I will know that while I might provide for all they need, it is their stubborn persistence that has won the day.

Life extends itself, but my efforts have only taken it so far. The seeds were waiting, but needed still to be discovered.

THREE

I GO UP TO THE NORTH COUNTRY TO FEEL SMALL

It's thrilling to run your hand across a
polished tabletop but it is even more thrilling
when you learn the slab of wood
is fifty thousand years old.

A Splintered History of Wood
Spike Carlsen

There are wild horses out on the lake today, what Sigurd Olson called the curling fog arising from Superior and inland lakes on days when the water is much warmer than the air. It is an impressive sight. Gigantic ore boats are ghost-ships moving through kettles of steam bound for harbors in Duluth or Thunder Bay.

The night sky is dusted with stars that reach beyond what is visible in the South. There, the humidity and lights of cities brush the heavens and tone down the piercing magnitude of stars beyond stars, their light originating thousands of light years away.

There are many feet of snow up on the Gunflint Trail tonight. At places on the Laurentian Divide, it catches on the elevation and dumps down on cabin-owners who winter there. The talk in town is whether they can make it in for a concert or pottery class. It is hearty stuff.

It is enlivening to live in a place where wild things can still happen, where mettle is tested, where we are not domesticated. While we have all the conveniences here that make life enjoyable and easier, we face the elements on a different scale.

The snow-clad hills above our town are a testament to the interior where things are written larger.

Here is the country of the wolf, fox, moose, lynx. Here is the land of the long silences that imbue the BWCAW with only one aspect of its grandeur.

In modern times we have lost this primal connection to the land, and with it, a sense of humility about life. We form it, shape it, design existence to our specifications. Occasionally there is a rift in our comfort, with accidents on freeways, something placed on-order, waiting in line or at a traffic light.

But to be genuinely humble, to feel small, is not something in life we routinely experience. We put ourselves at the center. This is a very different relationship with the world than those who have, for millennia, lived in concert with nature.

Perhaps the closest we come to this is when a blizzard sweeps down from Canada, and we are caught on frozen highways. Hurricanes, tornados, floods, fire can do this. These are things we cannot control. We stand mute in their path.

But to live each day with a sense of our smallness is what draws people to mountains, to ancient sites, to the divine. Awe is more than appreciation. It is this feeling of our insignificance that puts us in the world, in our proper place. It is a willingness to bend before that which is far more transcendent. It is to cultivate mystery.

I've been told by my wife that a lone deer has crossed the front of our property to make its way to our bird feeder, gathering kernels of corn that have been carelessly tossed by the chickadees who especially favor us. On cold winter nights this same deer remains in the forest but, occasionally, in the moonlight, it will come down to the shore.

This too makes us small, knowing we are protected by the warmth of a furnace or wood-stove. It places our world in perspective.

I HAVE KNOWN this feeling of rapt insignificance on the vast prairies of Saskatchewan. There, the immense space can be overwhelming.

From great distances, broad shafts of light stream down on wheat fields. Storms can be seen advancing from many miles away. The lights of farmyards can be deceptive, appearing closer than they are on bitterly cold nights. No one who lives there, or who travels through the prairies, can fail to be daunted by its scope and immense size.

The North is not a static place in winter, nor is it only geography. To see the Northern Lights scaling up from the jagged edges of pine trees, set on a ridge-line outside of town, this is grandness of another scale.

Here we are reminded that we are but a small part of life. The wild horses continue to run with the waves. The brooding December clouds on the horizon will not move on until they are ready. The banshee snowflakes in my head-lights, moving east on Highway 61, care little for a reason I went to town.

It is humbling for me to know I cannot outrun them.

FOUR

RAW BEAUTY

Where the gray geese race
'cross the red moon's face,
From the white wind's
Arctic wrath.

Scribner's Magazine
October 1908
George Marsh

There is a raw beauty in living in a country where open water exists throughout the year. In the long winter months, when much in the state of Minnesota is sealed, when long lines of ice and snow extend down the lakes of the Boundary Waters, to have the motion and undulating light playing out on the surface of Lake Superior is uniquely singular.

Wild storm fronts play across a hundred miles of

breakers rushing towards shore. Crests of avalanche foam fall towards the headlands, cruising towards Thunder Bay.

Winds rise up in Wisconsin or Michigan, and we feel their effects in roiling water, while trees stand against the storm motionless. Fields of boiling surf are cast out behind the surges of swells that, in many cases, are several feet high.

It is a sight like few others in the Midwest, the animating effects of open water in the middle of the winter. It invites the freight-train sound of waves rushing towards the rock of the precambrian. It casts away silence except on rare days when the lake is still. Superior is ever-changing with soft, muted colors of pastel yellows and grays. It can be hard steel on days when thick clouds march across the horizon.

Occasionally, sunlight cuts through the curls and awakens anyone to the spectacular beauty of this immense treasure.

For some, Superior's sounds are a distraction or cause for apprehension living so close to such a dangerous, changing environment. People think of sailors, unfortunates, their own insignificance. They are entranced by the very thing they have great respect for. And respect can occasionally turn to fear or anxiousness. Some flee from the uneven sounds of life here.

Others prefer the woods as a place of retreat, where noise subsides, and there is the profound silence. Still, it might be that instead of the quiet being welcomed, it can become oppressive as the long winter months follow in step, one after another.

Radio and television have penetrated homes along the Gunflint, and many living there enjoy this reprieve from the quiet of the hills and silent crevasses cutting through the rock. To walk outside on a star-cast night is welcome, as is the diversion of entertainment, voices coming from places that are foreign and distant.

Sound and silence, shadow and light, attentiveness and distraction. These all are accentuated in the presence of wilderness.

Their loss can easily be elusive as we become acculturated to the din of commerce and the whine of traffic moving along our arterial highways.

Silence becomes relative, but to know the profound quiet extending for miles over the hills is rare, and in many cases, unfamiliar. To know open waters in this same way is also exceptional and a privilege.

FIVE

DAWNING IMPERATIVES

For eleven childhood winters I heard the cry of the wolf, and then I left the country with no intention of returning. But the North has dogged my footsteps, and I have never quite been quit of it.

The Mysterious North
Pierre Berton

Pay attention to the things that claim you.
David Whyte

Sometimes in life, we don't have much choice. I know that runs counter to autonomous notions we have of our abilities to create the kind of life we want. I know that imperatives arise that are not readily dismissed.

In some cases, they nag at a person for years. In other cases, they are like impatient children who will not easily be ignored. They tug at a pant leg, or whine, or insist, and while we might continue with our tasks, they do not just go away.

On WTIP, our local radio station, I heard an interview with a couple who, against all conventional logic concerning career path, cost, loss of opportunity, and even health, determined to spend seven months in the wilderness.

Remarkably, the man had suffered from a medical condition prior to this decision. He was aware of the physical effects he still experienced. But recovering, he saw this time of venturing out into nature as essential to his emotional and physical healing.

Their photographs from this experience and the studio they created are a testament to this inner compulsion to act.

How many times in life do we ignore these whispers, these sometimes insistent urges and how much of our life is the poorer for it? While this man said he had lost income, he has a rich store of memories which will continue to nourish and inspire him throughout his lifetime.

Talk to people, and you will discover, even with successes, lost reminiscences of times when they did not follow these inner urgings.

In Saskatchewan, I remember standing beside a prosperous farmer looking over his herd of pure-bred cattle. He had all the outside markings of success. By most measurements, his life was complete. However, as we talked, he recounted he was the youngest of three brothers. By the time he was grown and ready to leave, his siblings had already gone off to pursue their careers. The war had begun, and his father needed help on the farm. He decided to stay.

Looking up at the sky that day, he said wistfully, "That is where I belong." Watching the trail of a jet far overhead, he spoke of his real ambition which was to be a pilot. That longing had never left him, evidenced that day by the tone of his voice and the look in his searching eyes.

When do we take chances? When do we follow our intuitions? Such experiences can be so compelling they never leave us, and more than that, they translate into other areas of our life as well.

One person I know who had guided a canoe trip to Hudson Bay in Canada continued to extend this experience by founding an organization specializing in adventure travel. All across the United States, his groups have traveled to wild places. Places visited in his imagination even before leaving on his first, great adventure.

Mistakes can sometimes be costly. We are all aware of people who follow these glimmers of possibility only to have everything not work out in their favor. Mountaineers who fall, business people who fail, talents that are not realized materially, ventures in love that end badly can all have unrealized endings.

On the other hand, to live is to take chances. We are insulated more and more from this, the possibility of the pursuit of happiness with no guarantees. As a society, we can become gun-shy. We withdraw or act only with the assurance we will be protected. We collectively can become timid and will play not to lose. This often ends badly.

Momentum can shift and go the other way. We might have a hard time getting it back.

For some, it is a matter of necessity to pursue one's inner purpose when calculations have been made, and there is no other choice. They act because the alternative of inaction is not a good one. There is more to be gained from participation in the experience even though its outcomes are unsure.

Imperatives are soft signals from some distant source that, because of our unique character, skills, experience, and place in life that we should act. It is not always pre-ordained — and we can refuse it. But, in the end, it is a choice we might take if we are willing.

Joe Walsh, serious guitarist for the Eagles, once commented:

There's a philosopher who says as you live your life it appears to be anarchy and chaos and random events, non-related moments smashing into each other and causing this situation and then this happens, and it's overwhelming.

And it looks like what-in-the-world-is-going-on. And later when you look back on it, it looks like a finely crafted novel. But at the time, it don't.

This is not to say his life, like mine or yours, is not full of many detours and things that were not healthy and seemed ill-conceived. It does not mean that there are times when we only have to make for shore and wait out the storm. It might not be advisable to do something just because we can.

It seems more an acknowledgment that whoever penned

the words "God writes straight with crooked lines" was right in their assessment.

That has been my experience. Life will order things for us where inspirations might seem chaotic or strangely out of place. It is not always what we would have planned. But it is, looking back, where we should have been, what we should have been doing, what in the end will have brought us the most satisfaction and joy.

It is to understand the degree of difference between necessity and acting on one's inspiration and following that call.

SIX

SNOW BUNTINGS

Can you bind the cluster of the Pleiades,
Or loose the belt of Orion?
Can you bring out constellations in
their season? Or can you guide
the Great Bear with its cubs?

Book of Job
New King James Version

Every year, along the shoulder of the road, headed up towards the Susie Islands and the border between the U.S. and Canada, there are explosions of buntings. These are small, white birds, flying in tight flocks that seem to move and sway with the wind. These tiny sparrow-like birds are only about six inches long, weighing less than an ounce.

They are a winter delight as they seem to burst across the landscape of muted pine and the occasional mountain

ash. They mix with the birch and white snow. One reference (allaboutbirds.org) described them in their symmetry as
a moving "snowstorm." This is how they have always
seemed to me.

The *passerine nivalis* bird, which is its Latin designa-
tion, is unique for having feathered legs or tarsi. Wikipedia
comments; "No other passerine can winter as far north as
this species apart from the Common Raven."

And winter north they do. Varieties of this breed can be
found in the Aleutians and deep into the northern outpost of
Kamchatka in the old Soviet Union. They can migrate in small
isolated populations to places such as Arctic Asia and the Saint
Elias Mountains on the southern Yukon-Alaska border. Their
breeding grounds range throughout the northern circumpolar
hemisphere where the cold kings reign and conquer.

And that is why they are gone now. With the warmth of
our spring approaching, suddenly I am aware these
delightful gypsies have now left the canoe country of
Minnesota and lower Canada. These tiny, presumably
fragile wisps of feather are off to the tundra and the treeless
moors and the bare mountains of the far north.

In fact, so encoded is the aviary DNA that they will
arrive at the high-latitudes of the Arctic "in early April
when the temperature there can reach minus twenty-two
degrees Fahrenheit, when grasses and weeds are usually
covered with snow" (Audubon).

And so we are privileged that they drop this far south to
migrate using the open habitat the lake affords. They are a
gift the snow gods bestow that we should not take for
granted. As with life, their coming is brief and their instinc-

tual habits, strange to us, are built into survival patterns that for many of us seem incredulous.

Snow buntings appear on the tundra in brown, ginger-colored feathers during breeding. They bear little resemblance, as with many birds, to their seasonal counterparts. The swirling, driving interplay of these small flocks blending into the flurries of snowstorms are temporarily suspended as they adapt to earth-brown, and the burnished copper-golds, and pale yellow of low-profile plants and grasses of the tundra.

As I reflect on this, I realize these tiny creatures teach me a lot about life. What we think of as fragile is strong and hearty. What we think of as fruitless effort becomes to them survival as they are awakened to the imperative of moving further north.

We sometimes think of comfort and ease and of the upcoming season that grants us more leisure and play. They drive into the wind and embrace the harsh environs.

They fly together, as one, for reasons unbeknownst to me, but I expect this symphony of perfectly choreographed movement and pitch helps too in their survival.

Chickadees are another favorite bird of mine, and I have always thought they are a grand symbol of the North. They stay all winter while others of their species leave. They are abundant here although, in the harsh sub-zero temperatures, they must take cover deep in the shadows of pine trees to survive.

But in spring as they appear at bird feeders, they are a part of an awakening chorus. The streams now breaking away from the ice and snowbanks are apparent. The staccato of water drops falling from eaves of homes is also part of this change.

Snow buntings miss all this. It would seem they have endured the worst of the cold. But now they move further north into climates that will test their physical capacities. They welcome it. It is natural to them. It is somehow right and in the order of things that they should stay ahead of the melt to wing their way hundreds if not a thousand miles to their summer home.

In some sense, they are the winter symbol for me that is coming to displace the chickadee. While the chickadee is a friend and companion to those living here, the bunting is true North.

THESE TINY, one-ounce bits of fleeting feather instruct us that our views of what constitutes hardship might be distorted. They tell us that a resolute mindset is vital. They signal that sometimes to leave comfort and ease is not only an individual prerogative but something whole cultures or populations must also be willing to do.

These explosions of white, flushed like pheasants from out of the trees, convince us that appearances are not to be trusted. As we drive by and see these snow flurries on sunny, winter days, they can tell us more than what we first suppose.

Snow buntings have left us for more promising terrain even when we cannot see why. Maybe that should tell us something about our national character and how we organize life on this planet. While they wing their way north, we are often content only with comfort. While they seek the harsh winds of the Arctic to make their home, we can value ease more than challenge.

SEVEN

WHISPERS

*A snowshoe trail on a sunny day after a light fall of snow
is a lovelier thing than I can describe.*

*Every individual print is beautiful. It is like sculpture and
like painting, endless impressions of a
craftsman's masterpiece.*

True North
Elliot Merrick

There is a different feeling for the land when you know the names of people who have settled here, in places you call home.

The vast coastland of Lake Superior is uniquely beautiful and rugged. But stories arise of fishermen and families in coves long deserted. They are just down the way, and their memory lingers as much as mist coming off the waters.

The John Beargrease dogsled trail, used in the late eigh-teen-hundreds and the beginning of the twentieth century to deliver mail, traces the shore and in places can still be seen. It lives in memory and imagination. On cold days the dogs are barking still, eager to reach places like Grand Portage or Two Harbors. Shouts of "Gee" and "Haw" can again break the silence.

This feeling for the land and its people is ephemeral. It is not readily apparent to those passing through. It is breathed into experience, more than history. It is that quick recognition someone is watching you without any percep-tible sign. It is that partner stirring beside you while asleep.

This connection once was more intimate in times past. Then, life was not so segmented. It was not unusual for rough cemeteries to be placed close to farmhouses. Parents would go out and have quiet visits with children too soon gone. Husbands would emotionally embrace wives here, under the shadow of a lone tree, to mark their grave.

Now we drive to tended cemeteries to seek out occasion-ally a loved one who has passed on. Then, it was but a quiet walk and a daily reminder, looking out windows past the headstones to the open prairie.

I RECENTLY MARKED the one hundred and fiftieth anniversary of the Civil War Battle of Franklin. There, 20,000 men died. Luminaries were set up in places where they had fallen.

Unlike the gracious spaces of Gettysburg, here land was

being reclaimed from old neighborhoods. In vacant lots between houses, candles glowed in the evening light. At another time, like fireflies, sparks would have shouted out from Springfield and Richmond rifles raised just as the sun was dropping below the line of trees in the gathering gloom.

I wondered, walking down those streets, whether people living in those homes would mark this day or go about the business of living without more than a casual observance of those who had died?

Outside there was once the thunder of cannon. Now, it might only be a car rifling down the Columbia Pike headed towards Spring Hill, Tennessee. Once there was the melee of shouting and insult to the wounded. Now perhaps only the sounds of parakeets chirping in their cages over the sound of the television droning on with the nightly news.

But many residents did not do this. Living there had not dulled them to the sacrifices of what had happened that day. They had not allowed themselves the luxury of familiarity. Walking in the golden blush of candles, their silhouettes joined with many others in silence. They too would have been part of the listening crowd.

We hear these voices and living threads to our past in memory as well. Places are not the only way we connect.

The wise, the colorful, the outrageous, the honest, those who have been present to us are all lingering somewhere just outside our consciousness. People from our collective past await our discovery in quiet moments. They come back to us and, for a time, our memory deceives us.

Out on the lake, voyageurs can still ply canoes bound for Quebec City and Montreal. There are still the quiet voices of men setting beaver traps not far away as the eagle flies. There are the rhapsodies of women working in kitchens at Isle Royale near McCargo Cove or Siskiwit Bay. There are the first inhabitants, wintering in birchbark dwellings, on the ground perhaps I too have walked.

IN A WORLD of concrete and traffic, of duty and places we must go, it is easy to think we are solitary. It is easy to forget we are part of this shared heritage, this continuum to the past. The links we have to those who have shaped us are often fragile and sometimes broken.

In this complexity, it might be well to return sometimes to a simpler environment where the sense of continuity to the past is more easily experienced. Here, on this piece of land, depressions in the ground between willows reminds me that once there was a barn or lean-to. It sheltered animals against the cold westerlies sweeping across the lake. Game trails might take the form of portages used by fellow-travelers for centuries.

Here it is the same wolf sounds, the crunch of winter snow, the wallowing moon coming up over the spruce trees that greets us now as it did to those early pioneers coming home from reverie.

We are reminded we are part of the mosaic of life, woven together by time and place. The haunting voices we can almost hear. Their whispers sometimes seem challenged only by the wind.

EIGHT

NORTHERN CHRISTMAS

*Let us spend one day as deliberately as Nature, and not be
thrown off the track by every nutshell and mosquito's wing
that falls on the rails.*

Walden
Henry David Thoreau

A cross the northern tier of the continent, in the places
I've traveled, there some similar features to the
terrain.

In Canada, the Arrowhead of Minnesota, in some parts
of Norway, there are collections of reindeer moss, rock tripe,
the same spruce, tamarack, and birch.

There is also one tree I notice in particular this time of
year. After the "yellow lanterns of autumn" lose their
needles in the swampy lowland where tamarack especially

grow, one tree says better than any other "It is Christmas" even in the frosty cold of deep winter.

The Mountain Ash, or Rowan tree, is known for its bright red berries that stand out like torches in a gray-white landscape. They emerge after the warm days of October, after the winds of November have dropped leaves on the ground.

Summer is not a time for the Mountain Ash tree. In forests I have known they take a backward position to the undergrowth, the alder and willow congregating in rock-strewn ancient stream beds.

In Bergen, Norway I have seen these trees clinging to the shore, bracing against the North Sea. Rarely have I seen them in the interior canoe country of northern Saskatchewan or the BWCA of Minnesota.

But now the moon is cold, ice piles up along the shore, birds routinely visit our bird-feeder and rush back to the protective safety of a nearby pine. It is the one time spirits are lifted by the bright red beads of color nestled into various corners of our woods.

THE ANCIENT DRUIDS had the idea that this particular wood was to be used for religious staffs. It was once considered as protection from lightning on land and sea. In Scotland, people would plant mountain ash by their door to ward off evil magic. Other places it is known by the names witch-wood or (my favorite) "delight-of-the-eye."

May Christmas have this same quality for you. Even in a place where there is little green, perhaps there is some hint of red inviting your eye to look, to study, to appreciate this gift.

Cedar Waxwings take the berries, bearing seeds from this tree, and will later deposit them in various places to distribute this delight-of-the-eye.

This Christmas may you also receive delight in unexpected places, brought to you by unforeseen people and circumstances.

May you glimpse the joy of Christmas even in winter grey.

NINE

ARCTIC SUN

I looked out at the icebergs.
They were so beautiful they also
made you afraid.

Arctic Dreams
Barry Lopez

I heard a new expression the other day. People were referring to the Arctic Sun. I had never heard that before. It means that the sun is as bright, the sky is just as blue. You have the impression the sun should warm you as it does on a warm summer's day. But it doesn't give off the same heat. It is the sun but leaves a person cold.

It is only when you stand near a window that you can feel its heat. Then it comes through and for moments, in the depth of January's grip, you can know the soft, gentle warmth on your face as you gaze up into the winter sky.

This is how many relationships feel when they are in winter. The sun might be shining, but it does not warm either person. The externals are too bitter cold. The sun might be too distant. Between them, these factors do little to remind us of summer.

We know this also as individuals. Everything should be right. We have all the contingencies of life lined up and we should feel happy or contented. But we don't. We are not warmed but are left wondering why such days can seem so cold.

Springtime is different (or living in another latitude). Then the sun's heat is apparent even though patches of snow remain scattered on the ground. I have been on lakes in late winter, taking long hikes, where sweaters come off and gloves are unnecessary. There is a joy in movement because one knows that even though the surface is frozen, spring is not far behind. The sun's warmth reminds us of that.

The Arctic sun can catch us in other areas of life. Stocks might be pushing upward, yet many may not know the externals or internals can be wrong. There again, there is the appearance of the sun that is so illusionary because the rising expectation does not match the cold harshness of what is occurring. Again, it is an Arctic sun that is shining on that particular shareholder's earnings.

It is little comfort to a person to see the sun shining in the sky but to feel little of its wonder and warmth.

It is a cold world, a harsh world. A world where survival is paramount and where frostbite can quickly steal upon the unwary if hands are left exposed.

The Arctic Sun is different from the warmth of summer. We should not be fooled by that.

We need to protect ourselves. We need to stop living with the deception that what we see is equal to what we can expect.

We need to recognize that while it might be a beautiful setting, with golden shadows on shards of ice catching the last measure of daylight, it is no friend of ours.

It is a precondition to the light of summer that will satisfy our need. But it is not something we can relish or experience unprepared.

We must first care for ourselves before we can enjoy the last fading of the day.

Covered and protected, a winter sun, an Arctic sun, can be striking and we rejoice in its glow, knowing that any other alternative (cloud and eternal grey) is a lesser alternative to what graces the trees guarding the horizon line.

TEN

SPRING WAIT

Only a mountain has lived long enough
to listen objectively to
the howl of a wolf.

A Sand County Almanac
Aldo Leopold

I t is becoming unsafe out on the ice of the interior lakes that stretch across the Boundary Waters Canoe Area. The snowmelt has created slush. On some of the surfaces, the white light of ice is darkening.

It is a time of waiting. Islands are inaccessible except to a few. Stores are absent of tourists since it is an in-between season. Winter is receding. Spring is not yet here. While we wait for summer, the warmth is tentative and fleeting.

Yesterday, the temperatures dropped, and it wanted to

snow. For a few moments, snowflakes drifted down and then stopped. The first robins gathered on lawns facing south.

It is a time of migration. The snow buntings blew in as a swirl and are now gone. For the first time, a loon was heard out on the big lake. Canada geese are back from their winter ranges but are scattered. Soon, the hummingbirds will arrive.

The dogwood lining the ditches and clinging to open space, with their burnished red set against the muted browns of the open woods, have been with us all winter. The willows are just beginning to open with their soft cotton announcing early spring.

The world is waiting. There is enough warmth now to be held for several hours each day. Light is extending, and the sun has moved far from the horizon line where it made its home all through December and January.

It is a restless time. People depart on trips to capture and to steal from spring a few moments where they can pre-empt summer. But often they come back to a colder world and a less inviting one. Time has passed but the season has not.

One writer, John Bates, in the collection *A Northwoods Companion*, writes of this time of year:

I have always wondered why we have April Fool's Day. I can think of no better reason than the absolutely foolish notion that spring arrives here by April 1.

It is something our whole constitution does not want to accept. It is as though we were bred, with the coming of the new light and the extension of the day, to anticipate spring's coming with a kind of controlled fury. We want it so badly.

Many study the weather reports of Minneapolis, or places that escape the lake effect of cold Superior as it modulates our temperatures. They think: "Why can't I be there?" or "Surely our weather can't be far behind." Last week it crested to plus 80 degrees in the Twin Cities. Here we rejoiced because temperatures came in over 50, which was a great day. Students were in shorts and tee-shirts. Today, it is hovering around thirty degrees.

The fading of winter is the time of year woodsmen appreciate being out in the forest cutting trees, hiking, discovering new topography with the branches bare. The snow that once was deep and furrowed is gone, and a few patches of ice briefly line the path.

YESTERDAY I WAS with a neighbor where we were able to walk the high ridges and look down on deep river valleys cut into the hills. We could see them so clearly now. Soon a canopy of leaves will change the feeling for the country as a whole. Mosquitos and black flies have not yet descended, and so we are free to roam unimpeded. This also is part of this time of the year.

However, these days seem to offer little consolation as the grey skies drift across the path of the sun. Waiting is anticipation. There is an expectancy as if we can get ahead of the laws of nature which will run their course.

In a culture that is always rushing, that has fast-food as one of its icons and frenzied commutes home from work as almost a national expression, it is rare to have moments where we learn to wait.

Waiting is a lost art in many ways.

Fishing teaches us sometimes we have to stop and put away our thoughts of what *must* happen to accept the inconsequentialness of the day.

The fish-not-biting gives us a new experiential value that is not measured by numbers or amount. While each cast is waiting and suspense, results too can be prolonged and not always set according to our timetable.

This doesn't mean we can't take pleasure in the deep quiet of a northern lake. We can take joy in the fade of sunset with the hours being put to rest. We can take more time to share our company with others.

These are the things we will often remember down through the years. These are the intangibles.

Other things remind us of this ancient rhythm we seem to have misplaced in an age where even voicemail is no longer fast enough. We text now expecting results within about 15 seconds or so.

Waiting for ideas slow in coming is one place we learn to have patience. Waiting for love, or to be loved, is another place worth paying attention to, but we cannot make this happen any more than we can expect robins to arrive on a particular day.

Waiting for important events to transpire when it is not their time is hard to do but what choice do we have? Events such as these have their own timing, their way of coming true. We can influence them, we can sometimes force them, but in so many areas of life still, we must learn there is value in watchful waiting.

Spring will not come any sooner than it does. In the first days of April, we may have garden tools ready, we look more fondly to our boats, canoes might seem more eager to be off on new adventures.

So much to anticipate but the time has not yet arrived. It will and is slowly making its march, but only a little each day.

Waiting may be nature's way of reminding us we have limits to our vital energies. While waiting is not always easy, we do what we can and let the pulse of time evolve as it should.

Sometimes, we have very little say in the matter.

EAST: SPRING'S ARRIVAL

The whole long day was a blaze of sunshine. The ghostly winter silence had given way to the great spring murmur of awakening life. This murmur arose from all the land, fraught with the joy of living. It came from the things that live and moved again, things which had been as dead and which had not moved during the long months of frost.

The sap was rising in the pines.

The Call of the Wild
Jack London

ONE

THE ICE FIELDS OF MARCH

*In the morning light, they realized their floe had joined itself
to the pack ice. They were trapped again, about 100 yards
away from open water. The sea was churning,
but all the men could do was watch.*

*We waited and waited, hour by hour, watching the wonderful
conflict of the elements, at times unmindful of our desperate
position, spellbound by the imposing majesty of the spectacle.*

Shackleton's Way
Margot Morell &
Stephanie Capparell

T he boundless inland sea is frozen uncharacteristically
this year. The ice didn't finally melt until late
February. This past winter has been historic. Not since

1971 has the ground fog of evaporating water, always present on the lake's surface, been silenced.

Great pressure ridges now make their uneven way out towards the horizon. The milky, glacial-blue hues, like gemstones, are present, translucent in the sun. Heavy plates of ice are layered upon each other. Each one is artistic, and together they are more than any artist could fashion.

Now it is early in March, and the chickadees are once again out and spritely. Deer wander the shore looking for forage they could not find deep in the forests above our town. The sun rarely is warm. But open shafts of flat, dark ice are forming out on the lake.

You can see weak spots where soon rivers of calves-ice will run free from their mother who gave them birth. They will grind their way east on sometimes unseen winds that cannot be felt standing on the shore.

Nights are still cold and can be loud with cracking out on the ice, like the sound of earthmoving excavators colliding. Sometimes it can be rolling thunder like grand bowling balls. Sometimes it can be the swish of slight cracks being cut as crystalline glass.

It is hard to believe this time of year the lake could ever be soft and pliable to the bottom of boats making their run to Thunder Bay or Isle Royale. We have experience and years of witnessing the change of season. But without knowing, wouldn't this seem implausible? Fishermen this year are telling us on some lakes ice can be three feet thick. While it melts slowly, eventually it will yield and fall into blue with whitecaps racing towards shore.

My wife and I and our two small children spent a winter on islands adjacent to the BWCA. Within a day the ice that had made travel slow and ponderous was gone. Black ice had been pushed by a breeze with the last remnants piling up on shore. There the sun made quick work of it.

ICE MIGHT BE nature's way of resting the land. I think of all the fish that are not pressured because, for the most part, the backcountry is quiet. Few, other than winter campers, enter places such as the Quetico and even then, it is only for days and not weeks.

Ice barricades prevent the unrelenting wave action from claiming the rocks on shore. While it might have the power to break, it also keeps the force of heavy seas away, if only for a few weeks. This year is different. But for most winters water relentlessly tests the ledge rock save where the ice has formed. There, while it is close, the water cannot wear it away.

Ice also makes the world a quieter place. Snow helps as it gathers and insulates. Cross-country skiers know the joy of venturing onto lakes where snowmobiles cannot run. There, for a time, it is the old wilderness, quiet as it was when voyageurs, trappers, and indigenous peoples wintered here.

The silence can almost be a distraction. But it is also a reminder of the tinnitus we face in a world too familiar to us.

Ice, in the 1930s and 40's, was essential to many people's survival. At Gunflint Lodge there are pictures of sizable blocks of ice being cut and hauled up onto shore. These were to be placed in sod-protected cribs, to be carefully brought out during the warm months of summer. Preserved ice kept meat from spoiling. Long before we had conveniences, this made life more possible for those living in the North.

Ice reminds us there is the coming of spring. What seems impossible is not. What we can't imagine is a matter of warmth and time. When we think of life, we can often be convinced the world is a hard place, where nothing will yield and where time is eternal and immutable. We can believe our horizons are one pressure ridge after another, stubborn, lifeless, where only the solitary path of a single fox might venture. Those tracks are not fresh every day but are reminders of how remote such a world is.

Eagles come and find a branch in some broken pine tree to watch over the silences, but they leave for better hunting grounds. They can survey and penetrate the forests where there is more promise of game and shelter. Other birds do not build their nests in small caverns of ice along the shore nor out in the carnage closer to open water.

But all this will end. Soon the thundering of great cracks being formed will be met by the lightning and rain storms of summer.

Soon the Northern Lights that play above the expanse will soften and be replaced by the soft blush of long summer evenings and a lazy sun going down past the pine and birch.

Soon the freedom of open movement will be ours again,

as we canoe the border lakes, or as sailboats set out, only to come back to safe harbors.

IT MAY WELL BE that ice is a reminder that nothing in life can stay the same, that hope is not unfathomable but grounded, that the one thing that is hard can yield not just to the hammer but to what might seem gentle, and to the sultry.

Ice is a reminder that over time, people can change, the weather can change, landscapes can change in ways that, in the grip of winter, we cannot imagine.

TWO

THE INVISIBLE HAND

*Tracking an animal is opening the door to the life of the
animal. The longer you follow, the deeper you enter into a
perceptual relationship with its life.*

Tracking and the Art of Seeing
Paul Rezendes

I n the Snow Crust Moon of March (Ojibway) tracks are
evident in the woods and along the roadside. Animals
are betrayed by the snow. They announce their travels and
leave their signatures as to what they are.

This winter we have paid a lot of attention to these
visible signs of travel. We have seen moose where they have
plunged into deep drifts. There are the etching of owl's
wings as they have graced the snow seeking out mice and
voles. Bobcat and Fisher have visited our neighbor's brush.

Deer leave evidence of their stay on moonlit nights by their beds scratched in the landscape.

With the warming temperatures and the ice vanishing from the rocks that line Lake Superior, the country is taking on its summer dress. Animals move as swiftly or saunter down the lane, but their movements are less known to us.

Experts might be able to read their sign and know, just as intimately as in winter, what the fox is doing as it leaves its den looking for food. But for us, we can see an occasional print in the soft mud of spring. For the most part, animals (from Latin: anima meaning breath or soul) activities are not apparent to us. What was once very visible in winter is now invisible. Or we can see only in small patchwork fragments, traces left in the underbrush.

We learn a lot about animals from the length of their gait. They tell us how big the animal is. They indicate how their uneven strides describe whether we follow a bobcat or a wolf. Some pads have a characteristic C written into them. Others are marked by an X made in the negative space between the paw pads.

Each mark left behind in the snow tells us of a tail that is dragging, a driving motion as they quicken their speed.

We learn that rabbits lead with their back feet that give them the propulsion they need. We know now that a flurry of tracks tells a story as mice, wolves, fox, eagles gather to finish off an animal cached in an unsuspected place.

Tracks are less apparent now. The animals haven't changed, nor have their travels been interrupted. We don't see them and are unaware of their presence.

Soon we will be driving our paddles into the water, and we will watch as whirlpools are created and disappear in the wash behind us. For moments they give evidence of our travels.

But at some point, the lake will no longer remember our canoe as it passes by.

What marks are we leaving on the land? What reveals our history, where we have been, what we have done? What are ways to explain the impact of our activities, especially if we only have fragments of information or if we are unable to read the sign?

In the larger picture, global change advocates would tell us we have all the data we need. But is that true? Is it the unmistakable track in winter snow or only the summer tell-tale of footprints moving on rocky ground with the occasional imprint only visible in the duff between the rocks? Can we be sure? Do we have all the information we need?

In our personal lives sometimes we can be as sure of our actions as the deer tracks leading across a tract of wet sand.

Sometimes we can trace where we have been, and we can know the joy of places that have brought clarity or relief or release to us. It is evident in the sign we have made.

Sometimes it is not so easy. We can lose any sense of direction as our path seems undefinable. It leads us over rock or hardened mud. There are a plethora of competing tracks that confuse the scene and make it hard to know what we have been doing. We have to piece it together, and yes, at times take our best guess.

Sometimes we can wonder why we leave the open spaces for the protection of the woods? Sometimes we can see from scattered scratchings left on the ground that where we are is precisely where we should be. We know what led us there.

Tracks are everywhere if we are willing to look for them. Our interests, passions, delights, compelling sights, our fears, and tentative aspirations or hesitancies mark the course of our lives. They don't tell us where we are going, but they do reveal where we have been.

Context is the thing that can make us more interested in what has happened and why. Mark Elbroch, the author of a beautiful book on tracking, suggests that "tracking is the meeting place between storytelling and science. Both are required at advanced levels."

That is also true for us if we are to look deeper into who we are as people, or as a society. There is a lot we know. A lot we can study and research to understand what is happening in the environment around us. But there is also much that we must put together in pieces.

We can surmise. We can take from our experience and what we can see to make reasonable guesses as to what we know. Storytelling is about taking the pieces of information and weaving them into a meaningful narrative that seems to make sense to us. From here, we come to understand.

In his book *The Tracker*, Tom Brown Jr. makes the point that each impression left in the world represents a thin, warm line between us and what is at the other end. If we follow it quietly and carefully, we just might get a sighting of

this living animal who might well be looking back at us —
sometimes before we ever see it.

To follow that is not to follow a hypothetical. While it
might be an indistinct line, we know it is as real as we are. ·
We know that sometimes life can also be as real: our calling,
the people we come to know, the touch of the spiritual, our
openness to the movements in the world. These can warn us
or surprise us with such beauty. They, in fact, are what
might be staring at us as we follow with eyes steadily on the
ground.

Tracking in the snow makes us so much more aware, not
just of the animals themselves, but of the natural setting
around us. Our senses are heightened. We take more interest. We too feel much more a part of the places we are
visiting.

In springtime we can still spot disturbances in the grass,
scuff marks on the hard ground, broken stems off of trees. I
remember at one portage the soft shore and the clear foot-
print of a wolf. Another summer portage in my past held the
deep post-hole imprints of a moose struggling to makes its
way through the muck out to the lake.

Still, we can look forward to another season when movements will be more visible to us. Someday we will be revisited by guests grazing in the moonlight that will leave their
visible traces in the newly fallen snow.

THREE

APRIL SNOW

Survivors always turn a bad situation into an advantage or at least an opportunity. "In seconds my whole outlook changed. I could do something positive. I could crawl and climb. Now I had a plan."

Here he was in hell, and he had just glimpsed redemption.

Deep Survival
Laurence Gonzales

An odd thing happened this week. It is the first week of April here in the North. But last night brought nine inches of snow. That brings our total for this year to 119 inches.

It is interesting the reactions of people in the area, and those 225 miles to the south in Minneapolis. Few are happy and enjoying what is being described as thunder-snow.

Temperatures are now rising, and soon, in just a matter of days, streets will be dry. But most people I know are in a surly mood.

Surprises are a mixed blessing in life. They remind us that sometimes we are not in control. I have been told that "what's good can be bad and what appears bad can also be good," but on days like this, it is hard to tell. Surprises out of season don't seem to fit in with what we think is "normal."

But isn't that the nature of unexpected events? Nothing about them is "normal." Rain showers on our wedding day we can't predict. We can't know precisely when illness will overtake us. No one can predict a snow day for school kids in April.

We live in uncertainty even when it comes to the future of our children and how life will play out for them. Snow in April is a good metaphor for life, for that is what life is.

We might find ourselves in a place where we belong, but we don't know how exactly we got there. Life seems to transcend the thought we are always self-determining individuals.

For me, I never set out to be a "marriage counselor." In graduate school, I always prided myself, in this age of having a defined niche, as being a generalist. But life continued to arrange itself, and now I am surprised at where it has taken me. I worked mostly with couples and relationships.

Is it the right place? I think so, but exactly how I got here is unusual. It is a snowstorm in April.

I'm told this is the way business frequently operates now. Instead of what they refer to as the "waterfall approach," I too move using the "agile approach." We migrate from one choice to another, and that reveals where we will go next. We don't know the end-game. We can't calibrate exactly, always where events will take us.

> We move unknowingly, like a candle carried by someone in the dark where we can only see maybe three or four feet up an unknown path.

Surprises are something we can rail against in April, but April is a month of surprises. Life is unsettled. We are moving toward the joys of summer, but we are not there yet. Life rarely proceeds from this to that, but often we wish it were so.

People depressed want it to be different — now. People who are anxious self-consciously look at every new indication of their anxiety, physical or imaginary, as something they want to be rid of. Surprises of this kind are always deemed to be "bad."

Conversely, there are also pleasant surprises. We receive amounts of money, and that is great if unexpected. We overeat some days and weigh ourselves the next to find we have lost weight. How could this happen? Ideas come when we have been stymied, when we have no reason to think we can break out of this dry period. But they do. Snowstorms in April.

We too soon acclimate to these positive changes that occur. We forget. Surprises one day become absorbed into the routine of the next few days. Strangely, we rarely turn back to thank whatever forces have bestowed on us these "blessings." We only move on and often characterize life as only having the makings of a machine.

SURPRISES LIKE SNOWSTORMS in April make us aware that life is not as conventional as we might think or want it to be.

They tell us, in the drifting flakes that accumulate, that we can bend to the wind and seek shelter sometimes and that this can be good, or we can argue against life when it doesn't conform to what we think it should (and must) be.

As with the waterfall, we can set our goals and expect them to make their way straight down to the bottom in unbroken and definite lines or we can adapt and move with the new challenges we face.

Yes, there occasionally are unexpected snowstorms in April that are out-of-sync with the seasons. As much as we think otherwise, they are part of the natural order of things. We can fight them. We can rail against them. We can resent their presence in our lives.

But there is also the thought that in April warm days will soon sweep away the snow. The cold will not last. The flurries will move northward and, in a matter of days, the brown earth will once again appear where now there is only winter white.

FOUR

BASE CAMPS

I'd much rather be here on the ground
wishing I were in the air
than in the air wishing
I were on the ground.

Boone Bracket

Quoted in Deep Survival
Lawrence Gonzales

I see them in pictures nestled on the sides of mountains in the inspiring swale of the Rockies or the Cascades. Tiny, diminutive tents where inhabitants are poised for the great ascent in the days to follow.

Here in the Canoe Country base camps afford very little value. Here supplies are freighted and accompany those who set out. I have known of few instances where it was necessary to bring in goods to be retrieved at some later time. For those on the way to Hudson Bay, sometimes seventeen-foot canoes need to be brought in by train. Here they will be exchanged for the large North Canoes that have transported groups across Lake Winnipeg.

Most canoe trips are not like that. Canoes are fleet and agile crafts, easily adaptable to most conditions in the North. While size restricts the amount they can carry, that can be a good thing. Portages come easier. It reminds us of the more primitive where we don't have all the luxuries of life back home. Canoes and the hardships of the trail have a way of keeping things lean and stripped down.

For any challenging venture, base camps are necessary. If lines become too extended, if one mismanages the delicate balance between too much and too little, there is a danger that those who attempt might not survive.

I think of the establishment of extensive base camps moving up the mountains, for example, on K2 or Everest. Gradually, these safe havens become smaller. Still, they are a place for storing up what might be needed at the higher elevations.

They become places to retreat to, harbors to wait out the weather.

Here, human company is enjoyed where radios can be set up to stay in contact with those supporting the ascent.

Psychologically, base camps provide a measure of consolation knowing climbers are not alone in a hostile and unforgiving landscape. They point to a habitation on the far margins of the familiar world.

In swirling snow and with conditions growing worse, even in snow ditches dug out to escape the unrelenting cold, they provide assurance there is a place where reserves have not been exhausted.

Base camps are also necessary in life if we are to be successful. Too many people attempt an ascent carelessly, thinking defiance and bravado and the will to overcome is enough to take them to the summit. They have not planned for the support they will need. They are unaware that unless conditions are perfect, they will fail in their attempts.

I think about base camps this time of year as the lake prepares for summer boats.

Back in the days of voyageurs, it was imperative in late summer they plan correctly to leave places such as Grand Portage to make it back to Quebec City, or to the hinterlands of the Athabaskan country. Once there, they would have provisions to take them through the winter.

But if delay cost them, they would risk canoes being frozen in small tributary streams. There would be incredible hardship and danger in not making it home. Perhaps some provision was set aside along the route to rely on if limits were stretched.

If you read books about the race to the South Pole, you will know that Scott approached this in the conventional European way of laying in large stocks of food and equipment to accompany him on his journey. Finding them in a seamless world of ice and cloud cover would cost him vital time and eventually end in failure and death.

Amundsen, on the other hand, embraced the traditional ways and lived as natives, procuring provisions as he moved across treeless expanses of endless ice. He succeeded in reaching his objective.

And so, we have these two imperatives where we must walk a fine and carefully constructed line: the need for base camps that can support us, and the knowing we will also be provisioned along the way with opportunities we cannot yet imagine.

In our planning, there must be some recognition we will have what we need when it is necessary. We don't have to know everything. We can't guarantee outcomes, but once we have set off, it is likely that some essentials will need to be there that can assist us.

Still, to embark without consideration for what will be necessary is foolhardy. Nature will not forgive the lapses in judgment, the naiveté, the hubris of those who think they can overcome by sheer force of will or imagination or blind luck.

BASE CAMPS ARE NOT the entire journey. Few intrepid explorers in this day, as well as in the past, would be satisfied knowing they had arrived only to set up camp. One does not stay there except to acclimate to the altitude, or to wait out nasty weather. It is not a place where one wants to establish too much comfort. Otherwise, ambitions might be lost.

However, base camps provide us with platforms where

we can venture out knowing we have the support if it is needed. There is a plan B, and moving up towards goals is an incremental matter of building a structure as well as taking chances. In doing this, we can move forward with a higher degree of certainty.

From perches higher up the face we can look down and occasionally see the infinitesimally small beads of nylon color that remind us we are not over-extended or alone.

There are places in a world of immensity we can call home, and, because of this, it gives us greater confidence in moving towards the pinnacle of our experience.

FIVE

Even goats may have starlight
in their eyes.

(Source Text Unknown)
Robert W. Service

I love that image. Think of all the other animals — the wallaby, the emu, the fox slinking through the night. Think of the cottonmouth snake, the pigeon, the deer crossing the highway in October's moonlight.

We are good at making distinctions. We think good or bad. Judgments are part of our scientific heritage. To separate what is different, to seek out the uncommon, to find the quirk or the thing that does not seem to matter but that, in the end, is all that matters, is critical to our race and development in the world.

Sherlock Holmes took advantage of this in *The Hound*

of the Baskervilles. He built his whole logic around what was *not* present and, at first, unnoticed by Scotland Yard. He solves the case by wondering about the dog that never barked the night of the murder.

He concluded, because of that one thing, it must have been a family member or friend of the family. This person would have been known to the dog. There would have been nothing unusual. No cause for alarm.

We depend on such differentiation. Science is often guided by these. However, starlight, even in the eye of a goat, reminds us that separating reality is not always the best thing to do. There are things we do have in common. Rather than being different we also have a shared existence.

I walk the town and wonder about this, and why people can seem so indifferent to each other.

> We don't see starlight in the eye of strangers. People's gazes tend to look through us. There is a protective shell we share.

We are told by their eyes not to look, not to be interested, not to even be curious about something that catches our attention. They keep us away.

People can do this even to themselves. They can forget they are more than ordinary, that there is starlight in their eyes. We don't see it because we can't see ourselves. Artists bring people alive by painting in that tiny bit of light in their subject's eyes. But from inside we can't see this. We can't see in ourselves what we often see in others.

Starlight is a reminder there is something glorious in the human spirit, in each human being. I wish I could see this more. I wish I could stop discriminating between the good of a wolf, their eyes shining in a photograph, and the plainness of goats; how casually I dismiss them.

I wish I could see that goats share the same starlight, that on dark nights as they graze, they look up to the sky in the same way as the snowy owl who gathers in perhaps more light, but who is in the end no different.

Starlight greets them both under a canopy of thousands of its cousins.

SIX

MILESTONES

Not all who wander are lost.

Too Soon Old, Too Late Smart
Gordon Livingston

Every day I try to walk my dog along Highway 61. It borders the shore of Lake Superior, and my dog reminds me there are new things to witness each time we go. Yesterday, a deer bolted out of the brush to stand on the shoulder. Its scent seemed to carry for a quarter-mile as Jack scrambled to ferret out what was already gone.

On windy or inclement days I seek out milestones, identifiable places I can get to, and then they multiply to more. These signposts are what carry me along and make life easier. To break it off into small pieces. To make the long road more achievable.

Milestones can help us to accomplish often more than

we imagine. It is a gift to our species, I believe, that we can do this. We can peer into the future, know or at least anticipate its difficulties and retreat into more achievable objectives. As time transpires, we can get it done.

Milestones add richness to lives that are often surfeited by too much of everything. They pare us down to what is frequently the one thing that is essential. They make us look more, listen more, be attuned when thinking of the whole would seem to be overwhelming.

I am impressed by a world-class photographer named Jim Brandenburg. He lives here in the North, and his photos truly are essays. He has taught me to look more for the particular.

Subtleties, such as a raven's feather cast on a bed of leaves, or a human reflection seen in the fading, fluid eye of a deer that has recently died, these remind me that life is a series of moments that can be singularly unique.

One of his books details what it is to be selective. He recalls, as a photographer for National Geographic, being given the opportunity to shoot hundreds of photographs in one day. However, for this project, he determined to shoot only one picture over a twenty-four hour period — for ninety days between the autumnal equinox and winter solstice.

Milestones everywhere, subjects of interest. Should he go on towards what he could not know or does he embrace *this* eagle in flight, *this* timeless solitude peering into a darkened grove of cedar trees? Should he photograph the shimmering gold of dawn being played out on *this* northern river, or should he wait for what the rest of the day might bring?

Each picture would send him home. Selections would

have been made. It was part of the discipline to look more carefully, knowing he didn't have the luxury of endless choices. Pictures to waste.

Milestones can sharpen our views and perceptions of how we look at life.

Milestones can also be missed. I look forward, typically, to where I am going. My focus is there, but when I arrive, I realize, sometimes uneasily, what I have been missing.

Where was I? Where had my thoughts taken me that I was so self-absorbed? What small details had I walked by, and what part of the natural world had offered me something only to have it ignored?

Walking my dog, I seek out the next objective and realize he is oblivious to this. Every moment is inviting to my little cairn dog and inspires curiosity. Every step has promise attached to it.

SOME MILESTONES ARE MORE MEANINGFUL. We reach them and should know how important they are. Otherwise, life is just a constant striving, and while it is true that life requires us to complete necessary tasks, sometimes it should also extend its benediction to what we have accomplished. I know people who don't stop to consider this. They never credit themselves and, like sharks, are forever on the move.

For me, my milestones are quite humble these days. To extend the range of my walking, to get to a particular bridge, or to arrive at a specific place along the shore — with greater awareness. Canoe trips are not so much about covering the miles or boasting about how far or in what part of the canoe country I traveled.

Instead, accomplishments are meant to be savored and enjoyed at each stage of life. While conditions may not be what they were, we can still challenge ourselves and celebrate when we arrive.

I LIVE in a land where Superior runs some 250 miles to the East. Canada's borders fling open a thousand miles to the North. The interior is almost limitless to one paddling a solo canoe. Here, milestones are an ironic reminder that sometimes things can be too vast to be fully understood.

We should, like that photographer, occasionally limit ourselves to making selective choices, to determine what is going to be truly important to us, to take satisfaction in what we have completed. Whether it is taking photographs, or in memories that filter through busy and restless minds, sometimes we can be content with our discoveries. They may not be the "one great picture," but they are sufficient for that day. Now, we can go home.

We should, over the course of our lives, come to know places where we have arrived before we push on.

Superior has always been awake, brooding.
Through the winter she keeps her secret close.

But it is in the spring that the subdued grays
and flint are lost in the sudden blue
and bursting sounds and colors
of new life in the North.

To sit and listen.
To hear beneath the crinkle of ice,
the slow, rhythmic up and down breathing
of Superior itself.

J. Bragstad

SEVEN

SPLIT ROCK: A TRIBUTE TO THOSE WHO ARE AWARE

When personal mastery becomes a discipline, it embodies two underlying movements. The first is continually clarifying what is important to us. The second is continually learning how to see current reality more clearly.

The Fifth Discipline
Peter Senge

One of the most beautiful parts of Minnesota, breathtaking really, is along the North Shore of Lake Superior. The road closely parallels the breadth of lake stretching out towards Wisconsin and Michigan.

And along that shore, there is a break in the trees. And from the road, you can see Split Rock Lighthouse perched on a cliff above the blue expanses of open water.

It is classic in its shape and grandeur, no impermanence

here. It appears to have been built to last, by someone who did not want something only functional. Here families would spend endless hours maintaining the light, looking out for sailors beset by terrible storms or fog.

It was remote at the time it was constructed. No roads coming up from Duluth. Only steamers, such as *America*, freighting brick and glass and those intricate mechanisms that would broadcast this great beam out into the void.

A friend of mine told me recently he had taken a guided tour of this magnificent part of our history. The guide had put the purpose of this lighthouse into context. He said: "If you hear the foghorn, you would be too close. It's already too late." And he added, "That sound can be heard five miles out from shore."

IDEALLY, life should be coherent. We should be able to plan for things that often stray beyond our control. We should respond quickly and avoid the dangers.

But life is not always like that.

Sometimes we miss the distant sound. We are so convinced things cannot possibly be otherwise. Sometimes we only have the intimation that things are not going to end well.

Sometimes we are so determined in our course, and plans seem fixed. It never occurs to us that trouble might be chasing after us.

One man I know, dying of cancer, said to everyone coming to his hospital room: "There is no security." The irony is, he was a financial planner and had done an excellent job with his portfolio. At the time he was reeling. He had not considered that the shore might be closer than he had estimated.

Sometimes the faint sound of the foghorn out-to-sea is something we recognize as a distinct possibility, and so we can make corrections to our path — sooner rather than later. We can adjust. It can come as a relief to know that the first inkling of its throaty echo, is all we need to alter our course slightly.

It may not always seem apparent to others. Friends may wonder what is wrong with the present, causing us to shift away from one path towards another. Others may think we are reckless or foolish to take our lives — so majestic and broad as freighters — with such momentum moving in one direction to shift to another direction.

However, they can also be wrong. They may not hear the first whisper of the foghorn as clearly as you.

Remember: the moment the foghorn is heard, that same momentum can make it impossible to turn to avoid the rocks waiting to pierce the hull.

Ideally, we all like to make mid-course, slow corrections that degree-by-degree can move us into a safe lane or passage. Sometimes it is better to do this farther from shore before things can become unalterable. Sometimes that is the only choice we have: to move now rather than indulging in the luxury of waiting.

I think of these things in my own life, primarily when things are going great. I enjoy the fresh smell of open water. I relish the night with its myriad of stars. Even the fog I appreciate as I am enfolded in its mystery and embrace.

But I am also aware that I must be ready, and make decisions now, to avoid the pathos of people who find events come upon them too suddenly.

"If you hear the foghorn ... " is counter-intuitive. "By then it's too late" is an apt warning from people who know the shore, who have witnessed shipwrecks, that stand guard but only to remind us *not to hear* that sound or to catch sight of the lighthouse beacon beaming through the edges of the night.

If we do that we are in good shape and just might weather the storm.

EIGHT

THE EXPECTANCY OF THE DAY

On this glorious morning, every track in her eastward trail was perfect. She moved in her natural rhythm, a direct registering trot, and I envisioned her gliding through the undergrowth, likely heading to the tiny wetland just east of my home.

I decided to follow her for a while.

Mammal Tracks & Sign
Mark Elbroch

Flickers came yesterday for the first time this spring. I discovered them doing what their name implies, flicking bits of leaves with their feet to disturb and perhaps harvest from the earth. They are looking for grubs. Snow and open ground are competing right now. While the outcome is not in doubt, it will take time for the sun to remain constant. Nights are cool. Cloud cover can make days autumn-like still.

For this reason, I decided to scatter sunflower seeds in the open spaces under the trees brushing the lake. I watched as they ricocheted off the witch wood and fell like rain onto the sodden leaves and pine needles.

I lived with the anticipation the birds would soon come back. But they did not return, at least not right away. I waited and watched, eagerly expecting their joy of discovery. But the land was mute.

We live life in the promise of what we have done and wait. Sometimes it is an indefinite answer. Sometimes we have only the future.

Sometimes we don't know what the outcome will be. And sometimes we wonder if the act itself has any relevance or value.

The expectancy of the day is what we humans do — and we must. Society is transported on the surges of imagination and ideas pressing against the future. It is what keeps the culture alive.

It keeps us from drawing back, from insulating ourselves from life. Foolish acts can only be calculated as such by measuring them against known ends. Perhaps part of our sanity, collectively as a race or as individuals, is in knowing we can always plan for brighter outcomes. There is something else we can do that stakes out future possibility.

For this reason, our universe can always be an expanding one.

Waiting with expectancy is the basis of all creativity, the impulse to write, to compose. It is to enter into the darkness not knowing if our efforts there will produce anything of consequence or value.

It is the reason humans embark on almost any worthwhile adventure whether it be marriage, having children, entrepreneurship, moving to another location, finding harmony in the midst of the winter of their emotional turmoil.

Sometimes we act without knowing whether what we do will have any long-lasting meaning or significance. We commit, but then only time will tell whether our wait will be fruitful or whether our effort has been an ineffectual gesture.

Societies follow this same path. In his book, *A Failure of Nerve: Leadership in the Age of the Quick Fix,* Edwin Friedman talks about whole nations that can fall into regression. Here, the two siren calls for safety and certainty come to mean more than a future of risk and adventure, entrepreneurship and challenge.

Countries become land-locked in their retrospection. There is no Northwest Passage to fight for, to move towards. Nations can become self-absorbed. There is nothing to animate their consciousness. Nothing grand binds its citizens together.

Whether the birds come or not, we must take risks. We must live on the edge of uncertainty and anticipation.

The Bible uses the word "faith" to describe this. In what is one of the most lucid explanations of what it means to stake oneself solidly in the future without measurable guarantees, the author of the book of Hebrews writes:

> *Faith is the assurance of things hoped for,*
> *the conviction of things not yet seen.*

Notice how what we want is already determined *before* events take place. Expectancy leads. We act by what we believe will be true and will take place.

Here many are planning for summer with canoe trips, adventures, the anticipation of warm weather, the opening up of the BWCA to travelers. The promise of this year is that I will fish more, relax more, care more about the people I love and want to be close to.

Many of these things may not happen. They are, in one sense, seeds that may have no more impact than those sunflower seeds scattered under my pine trees. Some will come to be unrealized. But no matter. The expectancy of the day is what lends to life its vigor and forward-movement.

Springtime catches us in this tension between what is and what will be. Those moving flotillas of ice pressed against our ledge-rock remind us that winter has flown by, but the seeds of summer have not yet been found.

NINE

THE LAURENTIAN DIVIDE

One ship drives east, and another drives west,
With the selfsame winds that blow.
Tis the set of the sails
And not the gales
Which tells us the way to go.

The Winds of Fate
Ella Wheeler Wilcox

There is a road winding its way up the Lake Superior escarpment that tracks sixty miles to the border lakes between the United States and Canada.

It is relatively uninhabited, except for the occasional moose, or bear, or eagle flying overhead.

And if you take this road, at about the half-way mark, your car comes around another turn and almost before you see it — it's gone. Most travelers pass it by. And it is no wonder. By itself, it is quite unremarkable. There is no grand mountain, no raging river. There is no waterfall. No landscape particularly worthy of pictures.

A simple sign marks this place. It tells the reader that underneath their feet they stand on the ridge-line of the continent. To the North, every drop of water flows to the Arctic sea. And if you turn to the South, every drop of rain, every droplet of snowmelt, tumbles its way down towards the Gulf of Mexico.

It is the great division point. It is a place of the ancients. It is remarkable, but few will stay more than a minute or two, and then they motor off, and the land returns to silence.

In my counseling, I once talked with a couple using this as an analogy. I told them that perhaps they stand at the Laurentian Divide of their lives and relationship. I drew an inverted "V" on my whiteboard. I wrote, "Forces of History" on the one side and on the other the single word "Future."

Which is it to be? With so many couples I am aware of the Forces of History that have built up between them. Arguments, discouragement, frustrated hope, memories that are not the best, all these conspire to take the couple perilously in the one direction. After a while, it seems there is a certain inevitability of things "going south."

And then there is the Future. I know it will require of them compromise, forgiveness, renewed trust, a decision, long-suffering and patience. It will require hard work to shift the direction. It will demand a choice.

Forces of History push the couple (or individuals) in one direction if we give in to them. And the streams that feed this are many. Family of origin means something. Was I loved as a child? Were my parents close? What position did I occupy in the family? Am I tentative now about relationships because of what I have experienced? What are beliefs I currently hold about myself, my future, my skills and potential?

These are questions we bring to ourselves and our relationships. If we have been wounded by another person, or have had a divorce, is it possible to think we emerge from this unaffected? Do not the ghosts of other partners potentially impact how we relate to the here and now? Can I take the chance to love again? Can I trust, when trust has so many times been broken?

I have worked with individuals who are, in some ways, a product of their past. Our failures, our regrets, choices made that influenced the direction of our lives can all haunt us. Anxiousness can move through the generations. Families can set self-imposed limits. They can dismiss our early accomplishments. They can dampen any healthy sense of pride. They can tie us only to our achievements. We can come to put these same limits on ourselves.

But we stand each day on the ridge-line of the continent of our lives. I believe we make "that choice" in a series of little choices. Our past does not make our present fixed.

I see this every day in people who are willing to go against the warp of what has happened, to decidedly move in the direction of where they *want* to go. These individuals have no proof, but they set out anyway.

They are drawn to the future. The Laurentian Divide for them is not something that happened in their past. Sometimes with great fear, with courage, they remind themselves they can decide differently, even with little information to the contrary. It is not always a spectacular place to be. In fact, it can often be quite an ordinary place.

In couple relationships, I can withhold appreciation or offer it to my partner. I can concede something in an argument, or know I am always right. I can look for the important places where my partner is contributing, or I can continue to fault them for their inadequacies — by my measurements.

Individually, I can summon boldness. I can commit. I can decide to alter the course of my life. I can reverse my thinking or amend it. I can choose to act differently, not because it feels right, but because I know it *is* right for me.

These moments of small decision take on larger consequences. We know this, but sometimes ignore the future and accelerate the Forces of History.

How about you? Do you believe your life is fixed? Do you think you've run out of choices? Do you suspect that decisions were made long ago and that you can't get them back? And where is it you want to go?

For me, it is pretty evident that I am drawn to the North, to the land of the "little sticks." I like to stand by that small, diminutive sign marking the Divide and imagine the journey a single drop of water might take. It joins with other droplets to eventually form rivers like the Hayes or Nelson, emptying into Hudson Bay. Or it might join the chorus of waterways leading to the Gulf of Mexico.

Even in springtime, alone and surrounded by silence, I think of the Land of the Midnight Sun, where for a few months at least, the sun never rests.

TEN

JOY IN COMMON THINGS

We should come home from adventures,
and perils, and discoveries every day,
with new experience and character.

Walden
Henry David Thoreau

My father-in-law and I used to fly to beautiful destinations, deep in the Canadian wilderness, up from the border. The accumulation of lakes seen from the air is stunning. Gleaming in the sunlight, the quilt of unnamed bays, creeks, straits, and narrows are all around us.

We arrive and the fishing is good, but I wonder how many bodies of water did we pass over in search of *The North* and the one big score? How many lakes, because of their closeness to the United States, are ignored? How many might seem just as remote to the person sitting there on a more accessible rock, the fishing as good?

In life, searching out greatness is enervating and should be rewarded. Some gifts are exceptional, places we should get to because of their majesty or unique qualities. I hope someday to get to New Zealand, the Virgin Islands, to return to Banff, Alberta and the Yukon. Norway, a place I visited once for ten days, cannot possibly be known in that period of time.

To get a "sense of the country," to do more than visit the alluring places, cannot be achieved in one visit, or even in two or three.

We can travel through, travel above without really knowing the landscape of the region or the people.

Sigurd Olson, a well-known and well-loved author, who enjoyed what was almost true wilderness back in the 40's and 1950s, portrayed this in his fascination with how much of the land is not experienced by those flying over.

There is the hardship of long days paddling, being wind-bound, coming onto blueberries in the middle of a portage path. The sighting of a moose grazing in some backwater slough, the satisfaction of arriving at places once only viewed as locations on a map, these are missed by those who fly in with pontoons bracing for splashdown.

The drone of the airplane comes and goes, and leaves

the land and those traveling there in silences that have lingered since ancient times.

Perhaps this is why places like the BWCA are so important, and why people fight to preserve them. Olson, in his books, always recognized that in the rush of civilization to find more, to move on to higher and greater discoveries and stunning new technologies, that we can lose eternal and residual values from our past.

These are a counterbalance to the day-to-day of urban life and dislocation from the land.

Wilderness can ground us. Time spent with companions in close contact, knowing the value of self-reliance and hardiness, the satisfaction that comes from concrete work and success, the joy of travel, these are all part of the journey whether by canoe or backpack. Something is lost taking to the air, covering in minutes what it takes canoe parties weeks to achieve.

This same sentiment is expressed well in the George Clooney movie *Up in the Air*. It is about a salesman who wins an award for the most air-miles achieved in one year but who cannot enjoy the pleasures of life on the ground. Later in the film, he looks up a woman he has met, who sat beside him on the airplane. He hopes that they can begin a relationship. But the one thing they have not talked about is the husband and two small children that stand behind her as she opens the front door. The story ends with a goodbye as he walks back onto a darkened street. He is alone once again.

I write about things closest to my home. Sometimes I wish I could develop novels, great books, theories that are beyond my capabilities. However, I do find richness in things I might have passed over too quickly or conveniently. Writing helps me to set down ideas and make sense of my experience.

Perhaps this is where I am supposed to be. Maybe the lure of what is "better," while it can be enticing, is something of a deception. It is an effort to cover more miles, but have I seen as much of the country that surrounds me? Have I looked at the particulars? Am I awake to *this* moment instead of in recorded pieces of time from my past?

It is also possible that in writing this, I have missed other opportunities even closer to home. In my abstractions, perhaps I have not engaged with things more at hand and right in front of me.

SOUTH: SUMMER WARMTH

The North Country is a siren. Who can resist her song, the soaring harmonies of bird melodies against the accompaniment of lapping waters, roaring cataracts, the soft, sad overtones of pine boughs?

Those who have ever seen her in her beauty or listened to her vibrant melodies can never quite forget her nor lose the urge to return to her.

The Voyageur's Highway
Grace Lee Nute

ONE

SWITCHBACKS

Do the difficult things while they are easy and do the great things while they are small. A journey of a thousand miles must begin with a single step.

Lao Tzu

When my children were much younger, we would head out to the Canadian Rockies for a summer of camping and hiking. Occasionally there was a vista or small mountain lake that could not be reached any other way than to walk to it.

The steep climbs were not easy, with smaller children, almost impossible. To begin at the bottom and to climb straight to the top would have exhausted all of us. Of course, that's not the way most trails are built. The logical "shortest path to the destination" was a false one. It could not be accomplished.

Switchback is a term we learned. It meant the trail would caress the side of the mountain in a gentle slope, sometimes away from our destination and then with an abrupt turn, we would ascend the other way. Like a skier coming down a mountain swaying first this-way and then-that, we would make our way to the top.

The Seven Sisters, Johnston Canyon, Mount Rundle, the C-Level Cirque were all beyond description. They were "ours" for that day with the joy of not being given such spectacular moments, but in knowing we had worked for them.

Switchbacks are something we should think about in life, and in relationships. We expect a steady pull to the top. Our anxiety makes us want to go vertical, the quickest way from here to there. But just as with mountains, that is not possible. In the same way, in life, it sets us up for defeat.

Sometimes we move away to go forward. It is counter-intuitive. Switchbacks teach us that.

Not dropping into an argument that in the past has only produced frustration and no positive result might be a good idea. Doing something simple with a partner when you feel like being alone might bring you out of sadness or despondency. Not forcing relationships, even when you want them badly, this may be the better way to foster friendships, a prelude to love. Exercising, instead of dwelling on depressed feelings, could be a way of gaining new height and more ground.

Switchbacks are not grand goals that put us in all-or-nothing positions. Climbing straight up makes us all weary.

We aren't able to maintain. Switchbacks are small-step advances we can manage. There are beginnings and endings. We can make promises to ourselves to get to the top of the next pitch, and then the next. We can measure progress, and there is satisfaction with each new achievement. Marriages need this. So do individuals.

Switchbacks provide places to rest. Our legs still burn as we move further up the trail. Breathing can sometimes be labored. Each turn is an opportunity to pause before we climb steadily onward. That is a good thing. We have achieved something. A goal has been met. Now we have a choice to rest or to go up to the next platform.

In couple relationships, or individually, where the challenges can be significant, when do we do this? When do we pause to stop, to talk, to rest, to gather our strength?

Switchbacks take us places. Most were built not to run us through the woods. They have a goal. Follow them, and at the end, they will spill out onto some beautiful meadow. Anyone who hasn't seen the Seven Sisters is the poorer for it. The uplift we feel and the sense we are stepping into nature's cathedral makes the struggle worthwhile.

As couples and as individuals it is the *destination* we strive to reach. Doesn't this simple fact often get lost? We can forget, in hardship, places we want to enjoy, the moments that make it worth getting there.

Similarly, summer days are hot in closed forests. But we press on towards a goal. Once reached, the memories of sore muscles and tired feet are gone. The trail is as long heading back, but we are buoyed by the grandeur of what we have just witnessed.

THE SAME SHOULD BE SAID of other accomplishments in life. They should have been worth the effort. We should also know what we are striving for.

Switchbacks on the way down stop runaway wrecks. Anyone who has allowed themselves to run a trail to get home sooner knows that if it is too steep, we will soon be out-of-control. The potential for injury is real. Switchbacks, by their design, make the transition back more gradual.

In our relationships, and individually, we need to remember "normal" isn't just the parking lot. It is where we are now. We can slow down, and perhaps enjoy as much the journey "home."

It isn't often in life we have to confront a challenge head-on. We can break it down, set reasonable goals, gain satisfaction in their achievement. We can pause to rest. We can eventually gain the heights and the position of the privileged few who can enjoy spectacular moments denied to those who think the climb is too arduous.

Switchbacks provide us a passageway to grand accomplishment.

TWO

KAIROS TIME

Have you gazed on naked grandeur
where there's nothing else to gaze on,
Set pieces and drop-curtain scenes galore,
Big mountains heaved to heaven,
which the blinding sunsets blaze on,
Black canyons where the
rapids rip and roar?

The Call of the Wild
Robert Service

Today was a perfect day in Minnesota, eighty degrees. Retail stores were deserted. The cashier said people had gone outside to play. People were enjoying the day.

This is kairos time.

How is it defined? Time that is rich, memorable. The

kind of moments we want to hold onto. Time that we *know* is important.

It is time you have experienced. When you go in to check on your two-year-old, and you see your child breathing softly, and you think to yourself "How beautiful." You stop to wonder what they are dreaming about when their mouth turns up ever so slightly with a soft smile.

There are times, with your parent or a friend, that are so burnished with yellows and gold and quiet that you think life can't be much better than this. You want it to last. You want it to mean something in the future.

These are times you think someday you might look back on and wish you had paid more attention to them. They rush by but, like old coins, silver and copper and gold, you want to put them somewhere to keep them safe.

People who have traveled in the canoe country can all think back to sweet evenings spent meditatively on a rock, watching the ebb of the sun as it drifts its way down. We can recall the echo of loons on sparkling water. We can remember the evening glow of fires, the joy of companionship, the damp softness of portage paths.

Still, we remember the hush of nights listening in our tents. Our senses still taste the first blueberry of the season.

The throated echo of the loon and the warbling laughter of their mating call come alive in our recollections.

These are moments we savor and enjoy long after they are gone. They remain in our memory, and many of them do not lack the vibrant colors of our first experience.

I remember a day in northern Saskatchewan paddling up a small rivulet on the Churchill River system between lakes. The sun was bright, and blue sky encompassed us all around. The route seemed routine, and then we looked down into the shallow water. Below us were tankers, great Northern Pike awash in the current.

While we did not catch them, I remember it still, as if it was only last summer. Their tails streaming back and forth to hold their position. Their dark, greenish, mottled color. Their immense size. The joy of thinking we might land even one of them. The glow of talking about it late into the night beside our tent.

In ancient Greece, kairos time was differentiated from Chronos time. Chronos is clock-time. It is living according to where we *should* be. It is scheduled meetings, appointments, tasks, duties of living. It is feeling the burden to "get there."

Some people describe canoe trips in this way. Articles are written journaling one achievement moving towards another. Distances are logged. Fish are measured by weight. Campsites are given scores on a scale. Even freeze-dried meals can be an attempt to shorten cooking time but to what end?

Adolescents often seem driven by clock-time. They wait to be twenty-one, or even eighteen. People put their lives on hold until their retirement date comes around. We target vacation breaks and hold on. We think about where we want to be (getting ahead of ourselves), or else we are in the habit of "killing time."

Kairos has within it what the Bible describes as the "fullness of time." Things will happen when they are ready.

Think about an apple. It falls when it is ripe, when all the growth it can summon has reached its apex. Then it can come down and is ready to be picked and eaten.

One person remarked today: "How strange it is that we long for the warmth of summer and then when it arrives, we sometimes wish it gone. We don't pay attention. We don't savor the moments we have."

Sitting on ledge rock beside the azure-deep waters of Lake Superior, I have wondered how quickly weeks would melt away, as I've watched from a distance the fireworks on the 4th of July.

Some might well visit the family farm for the last time before it is sold. While it might be necessary, and there is a lot of business to be conducted, few might savor the moment. We don't hold on and look around carefully before it is time to go and move on.

This often happens in life. We put away children's toys and don't realize this may be the last time since they are quickly outgrown. We are relieved to have them in the boxes and away, but an era is passing that we will not have back again.

We come across an old artifact such as our mother or father's baseball glove. It is a kairos moment that invites us.

But we often throw it back in the trunk or cardboard box as an afterthought and move on to what we had initially been searching for.

A mother's smile, the last glimpse of a friend leaving to move to the coast, the few leaves left of autumn drifting down in a breeze on the perfect October day, often we pass through these. We do not consider their uniqueness in place and time.

Albert Einstein once said that for some people there are no miracles. (No moments where we walk in the fullness of time.) For others, he reflected, everything can be a miracle if we see with new and inquisitive eyes. If we look closer; and look closer again. This opens the door to a profound sense of gratitude. We aren't owed anything. We are given much.

I WISH you a summer of these gracious memories, moments when we stop to appreciate the rare beauty of life. These are times we want to extend and hold onto. Times that catch us unexpectedly. Times when we should pause before we too quickly turn off the light in our child's bedroom. Times when we shouldn't depart before taking one more last, lingering look.

I wish you opportunities to stop and notice what surrounds you, even if you can step away only for moments from the tyranny of clock-time.

Whether it is in the pale light of morning or the firelight of a soft summer evening, may you stop to recognize, and appreciate what may well be the fullness of time. It may have waited for you until this exact moment. This may be the cresting of the wave when you will look back and say, "This is as good as it gets."

Then, we are no longer consumers, wasting time as if it was a commodity to throw away. We will be warmed by such recollections far into the winter months.

Thoughts of summer will come flooding back as we

enjoy the gift of experiencing things many times over in our memory.

THREE

BREAKING CAMP

Fulfillment is not in just having a lot of things,
but in relating with pleasure and appreciation
to the things of the earth that we do have,
without possessing them.

Wild Rivers and Mountain Trails
Don Ian Smith

Life is a series of breaking camps. Here in the canoe country, it is not uncommon to select a breath-catching campsite. Life is good. The rocky shelf makes for ideal swimming. There is a bountiful wood supply. The ground is flat to pitch a tent. The vistas are glorious. The night sky brings a moon up over the trees, just across the lake. It rises slowly as it sweeps over us.

But in a day or two, we break camp headed for another

destination. We could stay. There is nothing wrong here. But the journey calls us on.

Without knowing what or where the next campsite will be, we fold our tents, take up our packs, board our canoes and push off from shore.

There are many ways we experience this same phenomenon.

People who move leave one home headed for another. We often don't move away so much as we move toward. It is an uncertain journey in some respects. No one can fully anticipate what the new neighbors will be like, or whether our children will discover new friends. But we bid goodbye to one "campsite" from the water and paddle towards the far shore and on to the next portage.

Families join together to say goodbye to a loved one in hospice, or in a hospital room. Suddenly that loved one is gone, and we are left to break camp — to sort through all the things we will take with us, or leave behind. It is an awkward feeling, but an appropriate one as well.

As a marriage and family therapist, I often witnessed people who leave behind a way they have related that might have been comfortable once.

Circumstances have changed. Life requires more. The portages ahead demand hard work, but they have another goal now, and they are determined to realize it. They can no longer stay where they are.

Individuals leave familiar places to venture out. Retirement brings challenges as we must adapt and adjust. The ease of knowing where everything is no longer seems to fit the circumstances.

Children leave home. We move from one job to another. We are transferred even within the same company. We reach key bellwether dates such as turning forty or fifty or sixty. There are changes to our health, a rising depression, the uneasy intimation we are missing out on life. All these and more make us take more sustained looks down the lake.

We wonder. We dream. We think, "What if?" We spend more time contemplating the possibilities. We are more aware that time has changed us.

For people who are contemplating leaving the familiar to break camp, perhaps these questions might be helpful to you: Are you moving toward something or just moving away? Is there something to be said for the adventure of the journey and not just the comfort of the place?

Are your instincts telling you there is value in staying put? Thunderstorms and high winds can make inadvisable something that, on a whim, we decide because we can.

Can we be sure that the next site is not even more beautiful? This campsite might not be "the Best." The next might be even better. The uncertainty might trouble us and make us hesitate, but staying may not be the only, or best option. It is the same uncertainty that paralyzes action that can bring us new experiences, even more rewarding.

Are we overextending ourselves? Is what we are doing within our resources? Do we have the right equipment, enough food, the right people, a good plan? It's crazy to go on a forty day camping trip with thirty days of pancake mix.

How do we find the wisdom inside of us to know there is value sometimes in staying? Sometimes in leaving?

Breaking camp. We do this often. Life is not static. As much as we want security, it is not always ours.

And sometimes, in complacency, we crave the novelty of a new campsite in a new place, even though it may not have the same rocky ledges to dive from.

The fishing may not be as generous. But in time, the pleasures of this new site will take on a uniqueness all its own.

FOUR

LONG PORTAGES ON HOT DAYS

*Our ability to perceive quality in nature begins, as in art,
with the pretty. It expands through successive stages of the
beautiful to values as yet uncultured by language.*

A Sand County Almanac
Aldo Leopold

Most couples like the feel of open water. These are
times when they are in sync, when love comes
effortlessly, when they don't have to fight to reach the far
shore. Then, the sun is bright, and winds are fair.

It is the long, drawn-out times when we are discouraged,
when we are not on the same page, when love is strained,
these are the portage times when stress and hardship might
seem long.

Some portages are easy and relatively short. There are
others like Cannibal that are appropriately named. They

signal misery. The Grand Portage, historical and challenging to climb, takes canoeists nine miles from Superior into the interior.

Here, there can be swarms of black-flies, an occasional bee that slips in under the shell of the canoe. There are times when rock faces require you to step up two feet or down, equally tricky under the weight of a seventy-pound canoe and backpack.

The heat of walking in woods or through the mud, without a breath of wind off the lake, can be stifling in early August. There are always places along the path where roots seem to reach out to trip an unwary person.

Distances are measured in rods, and everyone in a party knows what a long, arduous portage looks like. Topographical maps show too clearly the elevation and how steep the climb can be. It is easy to misjudge safe places to step among the rocks.

Amidst all of this, there is one thing experienced canoeists look for and anticipate: the glint of water reflecting sunlight through the trees. Often you can see it a ways off. While you are not by any means "there," it buoys your spirit. And while the pack still bites into your shoulders, somehow it is more tolerable.

Canoeists now mark their progress and know the end is in sight. Soon, the cooling waters of the lake will be theirs, and they can slide their pack off and drop their canoe into the shallows.

It is then that a strange thing happens. The pain, the misery, the heat of the day, the length of the portage, the fatigue in a person's legs diminishes and is gone. It is forgotten with this joy of completing the task.

Now canoeists are ready for their next adventure, for exploring the fringes of this newfound lake, for paddling out towards the far horizon where a new camp will be set up.

NOT ONLY MARRIAGES but also individual lives can be marked in the same way. Sometimes the end does not seem in sight. We are alone. We are facing difficulty, and the burdens are heavy. Roots are there to trip us. We can misjudge the height of rocks as we step, where the ensuing dusk can make them more one-dimensional.

Encouragement must come from within. Many times, we move ahead watching and waiting for that first sparkle of lake light that tells us we just might make it. But we know that it doesn't come on the long walks when we are in the middle of the trail. We know we must wait, and move ahead, even when we are dealing in fractions instead of whole units of beginnings and endings.

For some, this may be a time of giving up. They put down their canoe and enjoy the false seduction of rest, thinking they can't go on anymore. They decide this will be the place they will stay, and that the pain is too immediate and real. It is *not* a destination. There are no bracing winds, and here the black flies gather in distracting numbers.

I often advised clients, "You don't want to end up in the middle of a portage path when the sun goes down." Here, there is little comfort, and it underlines the urgency to keep moving forward.

Some might try harder. They might work at it more, whether it is in marriage or for their sense of well-being.

Books will be read. Insights will be gathered. They might be determined to complete this difficult journey.

However, even then, people can feel lost along the trail if it isn't well-used. They can take a wrong path. They might have to backtrack. Their efforts can be met with swarms of negativity, or sabotage.

In the middle of a trail, when it is not easy to see the end, people can also lighten their load by throwing off a pack to come back and deal with it later.

In marriage and couple relationships we sometimes do this too, relieving our loneliness or sadness by having an affair or by leaving intimacy behind to focus on work or our children. Couples can stop talking to protect what they have. They can choose to "go along to get along."

Individuals can also relieve the emotional burden by substituting alcohol or drugs, by distraction, through sex, or redoubling efforts at their employment. They can isolate themselves. We find all kinds of ways to run.

All sorts of things are thought about when portaging, to distance ourselves from the bite of the yoke on our necks. People have been known to sing songs, to count, to notice more of the woods around them.

We may stop to rest. But, in the end, either we wait for companions to come back to help us or we must pick up and roll our canoe onto our aching shoulders to move on.

In our lives together and as we individually take on challenges, it means, while we might occasionally stop to rest and to regather our strength, it is the essence of our experience that we keep moving. We must set our objections aside and sacrifice to make our goals more possible. Not many come back from canoe trips talking about how beautiful the portages are; only that they might have been hard or easy.

Portages connect us to experiences. They bridge one accomplishment with another future possibility. They are only one part of the journey. Short or long, they must be completed.

They are a good metaphor for life. Portages must be carefully chosen. We must be sure we are on the right one. We must employ faith that this path will end in a right place, even if it is only now a configuration on the map. We press on, knowing while we are yet alone, we are making the necessary progress.

We wait for that glint of open water seen through the trees, which reminds us we are almost there. Our pace quickens. Our spirits are lifted. We relish the natural roll of the canoe off our shoulders into the water and look at what is ahead for us. At that moment, the memory of the portage and its hardship is gone.

Now the wind pushes at our backs.

FIVE

SOLSTICE

The candle allows the darkness
to keep its secrets.

Anam Cara
John O'Donohue

The birds are not the only ones celebrating. With the coming of warmth and the spring, hours of daylight are longer. The sun arrives at a different point on the horizon line. Nights are melodic until later, when pine siskin, nuthatches, and chickadees leave the bird feeder for the safety of their nests.

It is the time leading towards the summer solstice. It begins in late December but now is at its full height. We savor the days as we move towards June and the longest day of the year.

It is a different feeling than in the months of late

October and November. Then, light departs sooner. Shadows are more stubborn and persistent. The mood is of approaching darkness. It is a time when Christmas lights and lights scattered outside on porch railings or solitary trees in the forest serve as beacons of optimism and hope.

> In midwinter, we are not there yet but are arriving. If we can hold on, there will soon be this uplift as we pass, in a single day, from extending gloom into the first whispers of daylight, that now inevitably grow longer.

December 21, winter solstice, is the high-water mark of the year. It is more to be celebrated than New Year's Eve.

The coming of the solstice must have had a tremendous impact on settlers in log dwellings, trappers, voyageurs, lumbermen and fishing families all along the shore. Gone were the days of limited labor when needed duties had to be cut short because of the waning sunlight. Now they were free to fall trees, to break virgin soil, to harvest catches of fish far into the day. The night would not curtail them. Theirs was the joy of extending their work, accomplishing the required things that required doing.

Solstice has quite likely always had a transformative influence on the people living here. Among First Nation's people, it relieved the burden of ever-present darkness. It brought light to birch-bark shelters or ushered them out into their summer camps. It opened up so much more of the country since they could travel farther, see more, and know that summer warmth would soon accompany them.

We live with this same anticipation. It is a very different feeling living in May and early June knowing the world is not yet drawing down. Just as December brings the elation of seeing things are gradually becoming brighter, it is during the flurry of late June, with all its growth and activity, that we are reminded we are on a slow road towards December - and it's commanding shadows.

While it is not here yet, we brush up against it.

Life has few parallels to this, times when we know we are either on the march towards that which brings light or darkness.

We experience the slow inroads perhaps in either direction. But to name the moment when things turn is difficult, if not sometimes impossible.

SOLSTICE IN NATURE is a time that should be celebrated. I have often stayed up late that night in June to build a campfire to rejoice in this exceptional event. While I do this, I am also reminded of all the days in May and June when I squander the knowledge that we have been given more light each day to enjoy.

In the doldrums of December, I should also light a fire on the twenty-first to remind me I've made it. While it is not perceptible yet, minutes will accumulate each day and the promise of lengthening hours is inevitable and a certainty. If

I wait it out, it will come as sure as the dawn of every new day.

Solstices are reminders that, while time moves slowly, things do change. Positives are afoot. Even when life seems stable, we can be headed into darkness. At the blackest time of every year, there is a turning over toward the light.

It is a good feeling to know that in June there is still time to enjoy, there are moments of grace for several weeks yet. I should take advantage of these and not waste them. While days might all seem the same, they are not. Because they can so quickly seem to move the other way, each is a more precious and rare commodity.

The birds remind me of this, as they linger at my bird-feeder into the stubborn light fading into evening. The sun lets me know it is a different time of the year.

SIX

WATCHFIRES

*And closely akin to the visions of the hairy man was the call
still sounding in the depths of the forest.*

*It filled (Buck) with a great unrest and strange desires. It
caused him to feel a vague, sweet gladness, and he was aware
of wild yearnings and stirrings for he knew not what.*

The Call of the Wild
Jack London

Is there anything more elemental than fire, the lapping of
the waves, and a night sky fading into August?

A loon calls somewhere out on the big lake. Moonlit
mystics are at play.

It seems from the beginning these sights and sounds
have been enjoyed. The voyageur at the end of a long day's
paddle might have sat by a campfire, entranced by the

glowing embers, the smoke rising into the night. Men might have huddled for community sake, to keep the swarms of mosquitos away, to find some semblance of warmth in a barren land.

The trail on which John Beargrease freighted mail up and down the shore, sometimes as far as Thunder Bay, remains here as well. It is a quiet tribute to the cold nights, the quiet dedication, the persistence of the dog teams, the hardship known by most people here during this time.

For me, the cars still run by heading towards the border or moving south towards Duluth. They remind me civilization is not far away. Mine is not the remote resting place, thousands of miles from embarkation points such as Sault Ste. Marie or Quebec City. I have all the amenities only moments from this campfire.

The whine of traffic tells me how the landscape has changed. People inland wrest homes from the timber stands that once represented the interior.

THIS PLACE IS no longer distant. Still, the moon rises on the water, and it is as it was then. It is full tonight, and it splashes down on the horizon much like a spotlight on a theatre stage. Then, the moonlight disappears moving towards shore, diving until it leaps out again in glittering diamonds.

How much I think of the old brigades plying these waters. Suddenly the span of time between modern technology and the old ways fades away. For this moment, I am one with them.

This is the joy of life at its most basic. The fire I enjoy is not different from theirs. The night sounds of water breaking quietly on the shore would have been what they heard. The moon is no less full then it was then. The loon announcing the day's end must've been theirs as well.

All this is possible if we stop to place ourselves where all these images and sounds can work their way into the quiet places in our lives. Inside, the television is tempting me, calling me back to a place of action and diversion.

But here there are life's elemental forms and the peace of knowing I identify not only with the trapper but the Montreal canoeist, the wolf frequenting this shore, the moon's dance across the waters.

Here it is possible to chase a glimmer of what the past was like.

Here life stands still. Here the soft flame of firelight draws me in and reminds me that in a land of plenty, some things remain.

Outside the ring of the fire, there are campers all over the BWCA, with campfires similar to mine. Theirs is the joy of adventure. Theirs are remote campsites compared to mine. I think of them, knowing the silences are the same. They will soon crawl into their sleeping bags, leaving the night sky to drift from one star to another.

Their fires will burn out as darkness overtakes the land, as it always has.

Once again, for moments, it will return to what it was. Across the wilderness only moonbeams will catch on the bark of trees, the side of a beaver dam piled high with sticks, in the eyes of a walleye reflected some two feet from shore.

These all remind us we are solitary visitors, that we owe our debt to the past, that we are, like them, passing through. Their voices around the campfire are silenced, they no longer camp along the beaches. Their swagger will be but a distant reflection of those who come out now from their wilderness adventures.

But the land remembers, and the same rhythms are heard and can be found, even as daybreak recalls us to the land of steel and rush hour traffic plying the highways headed north.

SEVEN

UNINTENDED CONSEQUENCES

As we pushed the canoe toward our destination, the conversation was slow in coming. It seemed that our minds, like our bodies, had to be warmed into activity. So I do not blame Steve for not recalling from his French studies that 'maligne' actually means "wicked" in that language. Besides, three hours later, I figured it out for myself.

Distant Fires
Scott Anderson

Canoeing in Saskatchewan we decided to climb to the top of a rise to have a look at a campsite we'd spotted from cruising the shore. There was the fire ring with black logs put out by a dousing with water. Otherwise, the party had left earlier in the day.

But the fire wasn't out. Maybe 10 feet away there was a

widening ring of duff about 2 feet in circumference, hot to the touch, waiting to burst into flame.

My partner and I had to get our shovel and dig down in the cracks and fissures to remove the decomposing material — pine needles and the compost of leaves and twigs cast off in a storm — from the flashpoint all the way back to the fire circle.

Putting many gallons of water on that ground would not have been enough. The problem was *under*ground. We needed to address the situation, not in a quick-fix manner but in a comprehensive way.

Marriages and couple relationships that are in trouble often need to do the same thing. Partners can be troubled by an affair, and the reaction so often of the person who has erred is to want to move on. They are embarrassed or are recommitted to wanting their relationship to work.

But this can drive the problem underground. The wounded partner has so many questions, trying to make sense of what has happened. They distrust "reality." They doubt themselves and struggle with why they couldn't see what was happening. They are trying, often desperately, to reconstruct the events of the recent past. Flashbacks accompany them that are every bit as potent and dangerous as the darkening, black soil leading away from the fire circle.

Understandably, the other person is looking for a way to reconcile. But what is happening outside their immediate view is what might cause them to never enjoy a new intimacy with their partner.

In their reluctance and desire to run, nothing happens to get to the core, to discover the extent of what is happening.

They don't dig down. They don't think to trace their actions back on all counts to be rid of the danger.

I have worked with people who have learned to disassociate from their feelings and what was happening to them when the trauma occurred. It worked. It might have been one way to get through these terrible experiences psychologically.

Throwing water on the flame was one way of putting it out, and thank God they did. But the trauma traveled underground, and now it may break out years later. It can be discouraging and confusing to the person. "I thought it was all in the past," I hear them say.

BUSINESSES DO THIS ALSO. They fire people, displace blame, commission yet another study, run to data, intellectualize the problems, or ignore them altogether. They assign whatever crisis they are facing to the marketplace or some other external factor.

For a time, this seems to work. It alleviates some of the stress. It provides some semblance of control.

However, problems still tend to return or to replicate themselves in the same tired old patterns. There hasn't been any meaningful change or examination of where it is that the gears no longer mesh.

What leaders have accomplished is a quick fix solution, and sadly, even top executives blind themselves to the truth of their involvement in the problem.

They may never trace problems fully back to their source. While the fire might be out in the fire pit, it might also be elsewhere. But none of that is discovered because it is not what they're looking for. No one may be willing to dig down to bedrock.

> I think of that campfire and what would have happened if we had not been present. I see no reason why the fire would not have surfaced and spread.

It would have destroyed everything. Only the charred remains of trees would have remained. That island would have eventually replenished itself. Growth would have re-emerged.

It strikes me as odd that those campers, who thought they had performed due diligence and had put out the fire, would have moved on. They might have never known of the damage which resulted from their lack of understanding of precambrian soil.

EIGHT

THE COMING OF MORE

Talk of intangible and spiritual values
is never as exciting as evidence
of an expanding economy.

Open Horizons
Sigurd Olson

Sigurd Olson, in what I think is his best book, *The Singing Wilderness*, has an unforgettable chapter titled *"Farewell to Saganaga."* Here he laments the coming of a road to his favorite lake in the canoe country.

As the chapter moves along, there is the haunting image of the author sitting in a canoe, alone in the moonlight, with the wash of light coming from a resort that has been recently built on the far end of the lake. Here, it intersects the road. It is the only burst of electric light over miles of wilderness.

Out on the margins, he watches as the door swings open

to merry travelers coming out into the night air. A power-boat races by unaware of his presence, its familiar green and red running lights disappearing under a banner of stars. Eventually, he turns back toward his campsite with a mixture of feelings.

He knows what the gift of laughter and good company and modernization can be to those used to solitary places. But, he is also aware that everything now is changed with the coming of development and the amenities of urban life. The intangibles of old wilderness are fading.

We had a zip line, once considered as development, in the hills above our town. These gentle slopes lined with birch and pine were a backdrop to children playing and sports competitions. There is now a scar from excavators who leveled the site. It might have one day been profitable. I'm sure it would have been a draw for some coming up from the cities to the south. It would have been entertainment and something to do.

But what happens when the ridge-line is broken by the frenetic activities of cars and trucks making their way to the top, carefree tourists and locals cruising down long cable lines over the town? The dignity of the hills would now have been converted to use, but something would also be lost.

A popular program, *Gold Rush*, leaves me with this same feeling. For one-hundred years the Yukon has been a place of extraction. But in the long reach of time, it is also a place where eternal rhythms were once more apparent in the moaning of the wind, the silence, the unknown, the inde-finables that draw people to the land.

Ravi Zacharias in one of his books writes: "Where does

one find replenishment and ultimate meaning, especially in a world that mass-markets numerous paths to the truth?"

It is a good question and a timely one. He further states: "The danger here is that we often mistake relevance for truth and make truth so academic that it seems to have become irrelevant." This, I believe, is what Olson was reflecting on that night on the water.

IT STRIKES me we take a lot from the world. But while we gain much from this, we are also losing. I see many harassed people at the grocery store where I shop. In traffic, I am more impressed by people who want me out of the way so they can get home. We have children in an abundance of activities and planned events, but are they, or we, any happier? I have worked with executives who claim they have to work fifty to sixty hours a week or more, and the tyranny of their cell phones, text messages and emails would confirm this.

The old values are coming down and are being replaced. It might all seem relevant and vital, but truth has become blurred. Our pace through life might be disjointed, in stutter-step with how we have evolved over eons of time. But we might never realize this.

William Blake echoed these thoughts when he wrote:

> *This life's five windows of the soul*
> *Distorts the Heavens from pole to pole,*
> *And leads you to believe a lie,*

when you see with,
not through the eye.

The world is so full of distractions and activities that seem to compel us to involvement. But Blake, like Sigurd Olson and Zacharius, is pointing towards something more difficult, but in the end more sustaining. The ability to see through eyes to a world fraught with meaning.

Many years ago, I wrote the following one night, from a campsite in Northern Saskatchewan. I called it *NightSounds.*

Moon-swept
Night magic
Awash in silence,
Bending to the Day.

Eternal, Whisperer
Of the Dawn:
Tantalizing Daylight
From her Bed.

Hushed Woodwinds
Accompanying the Breezes,
Brushing the trees
With familiar accent.

Ancient Interpreter,
Mystic, Medicine Man
Moon.

The Drumbeat of Creation
Walking among the Hills.
Soft, serene, silver-tipped
Wings.
Stalking the Unseen

Mystery
Distant
Horizon-grasped.

Many things have come between myself and that moment, but I remember it still. The hush. The quiet, sitting on the doorstep of the unknown. The night painted by stars, and an owl hooting at me across the lake. I ask myself: Would I have written this apart from that particular place?

"Farewell to Saganaga" is a reminder to us that with the coming of more, we are not just adding one thing but perhaps we are displacing many more of the intangibles.

Do we see through our eyes a world we want, or are we attracted only by all that we see? Have the elemental aspects of life been blurred by what *seems* non-negotiable to the point we don't even realize? Are we substituting activity for meaning? Are we listening to those who define truth for us?

Are we only doing things that seem relevant because they appear to us as the most immediate?

I was privileged to work at a canoe camp where I would watch from the islands as cars deposited campers at the landing. These were adults who had raced up from the city and were now racing to conform to a non-existent schedule, already behind.

I know eventually, with the pace of travel, canoes would bring them back into themselves. For a few days, they would enjoy a quieter, slower rhythm.

They would pay more attention to the land. Their laughter would generate from shared experiences.

The land would bring them back in touch with themselves and the "deep, irrepressible spiritual hungers" that lie, often dormant or ignored, within each of us.

NINE

BLUEBERRY HARVEST

*Many a forenoon have I stolen away, preferring to spend thus
the most valued part of the day; for I was rich if not in money,
in sunny hours and summer days, and spent them lavishly.*

Walden
Henry David Thoreau

I n the North country, blueberries are not something to be
taken for granted. But this summer was bountiful. It
rained regularly. The sun favored us with beautiful powder-
blue berries.

Paths lined their way on up the hill through the underbrush. Most of the blueberry bushes had been picked over.
But my companion and I noticed at this time of year, when
the August sun is hot and days are long, that the best berries
seemed to grow in the shade, behind some rock, or in the
crook of another bush.

My partner informed me that several weeks earlier, my four-year-old grandson had been here, and, with each discovery, he would shout out: "Hey! I found the mother-lode!" Blueberry picking is not for the faint-of-heart, or for the timid.

Several years before there had been a fire that had roared through this place, on both sides of the road. It had taken almost everything. It seared the rocks. Blackened spruce, like sentinels, stripped of their branches, were the only thing left that watched over the horizon.

Many in town had mourned this loss. Many of the white pine had come down in the same fire. These giants, remnants of the logging days, had always welcomed visitors to this land of adventure. They were there when my parents honeymooned here some seventy years ago. Now, it was broken ground. But seedlings were beginning to show promise. The land was starting to heal. It had become a place of surprises.

This is what the blueberry harvest was telling me. We write things off while nature is already writing a new story.

We grieve, but already the land is in repair. We express unhappiness that things are not the same. But nature wants to applaud.

This is not a jack pine forest like the ones to the South, but they deliver the same message. Fire scorches everything.

But at a specific temperature, seed pods break open. Fierce heat is *required* for them to burst and begin the cycle of new growth.

We conserve, withhold, guard, protect, sometimes over-manage places that hold great beauty. We take a dark view of change. We mourn that things will not be the same. But sometimes the old growth hinders the development of what is new. Berries do not grow where the sun cannot penetrate. Animals will not return to places that have no forage.

Life can be scarred like this forest. We can view our pain and the often terrible things that happen to us and see only a moonscape, harsh, barren, dismally empty.

Words like "a write-off" and "desolate" and "a wasteland" and "useless" come to mind. But blueberries grow even as we recoup from the damage.

No one would expect this.

We don't. But sometimes out of broken ground, life surprises us. It is a moment of grace.

What else can we learn? Sometimes we look for berries in the shade, and they can be bountiful — in places we ordinarily might not have sought out. The best picking is often near the exposed rock that shows the scars of the firestorm.

Sometimes, if there are bears about, we settle for less.

Sometimes we know that even though picking berries takes a long time, that their sweet, wild taste is worth it, and that this, in itself, is enough to go on in the hot summer sun.

Life can be like a treasure hunt where, on quite ordinary days, we can still happen upon some patch of goodness that surprises us, where we can say, "Hey, I found the motherlode!"

Sometimes something as terrible as fire can sweep across the land and burst open the seeds of something entirely new that has been waiting for their day.

TEN

THE MYSTERIOUS

*We have our hearts in the right place,
but we do not yet recognize
the small cogs and wheels.*

A Sand Country Almanac
Aldo Leopold

That particular fish came down on my barb hard. I know, because in the stormy waters of Long Lake we fought each other for a long time.

It was the kind of day I didn't expect to catch fish. I hadn't caught anything. The wind blew in hard from the North across the sweep of open water — maybe for a mile or more. The waves were being unkind. I was in a half-bay, thinking more about controlling my motor than my line.

I didn't know much then about fish or how to catch them. There were no depth finders, no pros teaching me on

TV, or videos about the secrets that now are common knowledge.

The clouds scudded towards my boat, a small 14 foot aluminum with a ten horse chugging along behind me, breathing water. I was alone, not the kind of day others would want. I wondered why I was out there, the wind gnawing at my face and clenching at my exposed hands.

I took a lazy, slow circle headed towards shore from out in the flats, and then it hit. I knew it was big. I knew I might never, in my whole childhood, hook such a fish as this again. It would never be better than this on Long Lake.

IN THE DANCE between reeling and drag, I made progress, but I never saw the flash of brown of a colossal walleye or the mottled green of a great northern pike. In an instant, it was gone. The line had broken. I was alone again with the tingle of expectation, the joy of great accomplishment, the frustration of loss, my adrenaline, the devastation of disappointment, the chasing after images of what might have been.

It was a great moment. It was a sad one. But more importantly, it was the moment in fishing I will never forget. That moment happened over 50 years ago.

Why do we fish? I know I've lived in Canada where the abundance of catches is wrist-numbing.

I remember one camping trip we got lucky. Just off our campsite, we discovered an underwater weed-bed that was a fortune in hungry fish. For hours we circumnavigated and caught walleye that gleamed with the golden sun. Hooks were barbless, so we easily flipped them off, and the fish dropped back into the water and swam away.

It was a place we would always come back to. It evoked memories of our time in this beautiful country.

But this was one of many pictures that, no matter how much we would recall, did not compare to what I experienced earlier in life.

Numbers can overwhelm us, but they can also satiate us. After a while, they can become expected and ordinary. The two pound plus class of pickerel we discovered to the North in such numbers no longer seemed remarkable to us. Wouldn't our counting of fish that day have told you that? They had become a commodity.

Robert Service, the poet of the Klondike gold rush who captured perhaps best the underlying themes of why people pursued such wealth and endured such hardship, said in his poem *Spell of the Yukon*:

> *I wanted the gold, and I sought it;*
> *I scrabbled and mucked like a slave.*
> *Was it famine or scurvy—I fought it;*
> *I hurled my youth into a grave.*

> *I wanted the gold, and I got it—*
> *Came out with a fortune last fall,—*
> *Yet somehow life's not what I thought it,*
> *And somehow the gold isn't all.*

This expresses it best for me. It's not the fish and it's not just the capture. There is something more intrinsic and personal.

Big fish live in big water. But sometimes we need to be reminded that we can't quantify everything that comes our way.

I look at big boats headed up the highway on 61 towards the border country, and I wonder what chance the fish have? Down-riggers protrude like branches. Trolling motors, the command of 200 horses, GPS that can mark every rock-pile, sonar that paints pictures of the bottom that are three-dimensional all conspire to reveal the fish's hiding place.

We now know their habits, the exact levels of where they suspend. We know habitat. We can "see" them with (what singer/songwriter Stan Rogers described as) "long-seeing eyes." But we can't make the fish bite.

In this age of technology, where there are few surprises, there is still the one fish we cannot catch with all our knowledge. We can hope to find it but, other than an unusually broad slash on our fish-finder, it is mystery and a gift when we happen upon one that is exceptional.

Fishermen know this. Think about the last time you felt that heavy pull and knew something big was on the line.

There was that moment of waiting while you peered into the dark waters searching intently for that first sign. There was mystery, joy, accomplishment, acknowledgment, all waiting. It is the moment before realization.

I love the movie *Grumpy Old Men* where the entire film is premised on the one fish that is elusive and impossible to catch. A whole mythology is created around it, in the boats of old fishermen who know it is there, but who cannot capture it. They spend their lives trying, and the more they fail, the greater their respect.

"Catfish Hunter," they say, is cagey, wise, smart, careful,

experienced. It knows stuff. It has bettered many, and like a feared bull at a rodeo, they know it will always be more the exception than the rule if they stay on and can hold him for more than 8 seconds.

Why do they do this? Why search when other fish can more easily be purchased with a worm and a hook. Because it is "not the gold" as Robert Service writes. The point is, they might not expect to capture Catfish Hunter, but it is worth the noble effort, this pursuit of mystery. Catching, or even having it on the line, is something granted to them, not deserved.

That word "deserved," with a great fish, would never seem appropriate.

Today, the ethic is different. When mystery was common people would take a twenty-year-old fish from the water and claim it on a trophy wall. Or they would take it back with them and trim it into pieces for frying.

Now we recognize there are not many places left where instrumentation cannot penetrate. The elusiveness of places like the BWCAW we protect because, at some level, we appreciate the silences, the stretches of open space, the loons' call as it echoes across the canyons at twilight.

As we release these great leviathans back into the water, we acknowledge they belong to the unexpected.

We return them so we can perhaps one day come back and be granted a second audience. And if we don't get it, it is not so important. We catch that fish many times over the years in our dreams.

It turns out, in the end, I am glad I never even got a glimpse of that great fish swimming below my boat. Its length is not limited by what the sun could touch. I don't have a scale to weigh it, or a tape to compare it to other fish I have boated.

There will always be mystery, in what might have been, in what lies below, in what that fish did with its earned liberty. And why I got a chance that day, as naive as I was, to join with that moment — one of the greatest of my young life.

For me, that fish will always be there. It reminds me there are things I cannot know, surprises I cannot always anticipate, moments where I don't see everything, and places in the world where on windy, cold-to-the-bone days, magic and mystery might still occur.

ENDNOTES

Frontispiece

Pierre Berton, *The Mysterious North: Encounters With the Canadian Frontier*, (McClelland & Stewart Inc: Toronto, 1989), p. 22.

AUTUMN

Irene Stanley, as cited in the book *Distant Fires* by Scott Anderson (Pfeifer-Hamilton Publishers, Duluth: Versa Press, 1990), p. 103.

The Stalking Moon

1. Sigurd F. Olson, *Listening Point* (Alfred A. Knopf, New York, 1972), p. 15. From "Bearberry Lodge."

2. Ojibwe Dictionary,
http://www.ojibwe.org/home/episode6_dictionary.html
3. Don Ian Smith, *By the River of No Return* (Abingdon Press, Nashville / New York, 1967), pp. 36-40. From "Snow in the High Country."

Reaching for the Light

Epictetus. *Enchiridion*, trans. George Long, (Prometheus Books, New York, 1991).

Shoulder Season

Sigurd F. Olson, *Of Time and Place* (Alfred A. Knopf, New York, 1982), p. 32. From "Mavericks."

Wood Shed

Robert Service, *Collected Poems of Robert Service* (G.P. Putnam's Sons, New York: Penguin Group, 1921), p. 266. From "Song of the Camp-Fire."

Days of Brazen Color

Aldo Leopold, *A Sand County Almanac* (A Sierra Club / Ballantine Book, New York: Oxford University Press, 1966), p. 158.

Superior: First Light

1. Kevin Crossley-Holland, *The Norse Myths*, (Pantheon Books, New York: Random House, Inc., 1980) p. 146.
2. Wallace Stegner, *Marking the Sparrow's Fall: The Making of the American West* (Holt Paperbacks, New York: Henry Holt and Company, 1992).
3. Stephen Fearing (Canadian songwriter and musician), *The Assassin's Apprentice* (True North, 1993). From "The Longest Road."
4. Frazier Cain, *Universe Today,*http://www.universe today.com/26623/how-fast-does-the-earth-rotate/, May 20, 2013.)
5. *StarDate,* (https://stardate.org/astro-guide/faqs how-fast-earth-moving-through-space, August 11, 2015.)

Forest Undercover
Revised Standard Version: The Holy Bible (Harper and Brothers, New York: 1952)

Rivers Run Dry

Carlos G. Valles, S.J., *Mastering Sadhana*, (An Image Book, New York: Doubleday,1988), p. 142. From "An Eastern Christian Speaks of Prayer" by Anthony de Mello.

Chik-Wauk

1. Don Ian Smith, *By the River of No Return* (Abingdon Press, Nashville / New York, 1967), p 14. From "By the River of No Return."
2. Chik-Wauk. For more information on this excellent

resource at the end of the Gunflint Trail, go to http://chik-wauk.com.

WINTER

Roland Huntford, *The Last Place on Earth: Scott and Amundsen's Race to the South Pole* (The Modern Library, New York: Random House, 1999), pp. 364-365.

Snow Bunting

1. Paul David Dunn & Robert Schuller, *The New Possibility Thinkers Bible* / New King James Version (Thomas Nelson, Inc.: Nashville, 1996), Job 38:31-32.
2. Cornell Lab of Ornithology, (Cornell University. Ithaca, New York, 2014), http://www.allaboutbirds.org/guide/Snow_Bunting/lifehistory uses this description of snow buntings as "snowstorms."
3. Wikipedia, (https://en.wikipedia.org/wiki/Snow_bunting.) Inclusive of all the information in this essay on the snow bunting. This remarkable bird (sometimes called a "snowflake") was also prolific in Continental Europe during the last glacial period dating some twelve thousand years ago.
4. National Audubon Society, Inc (2015), http://www.audubon.org/field-guide/bird/snow-bunting.

The Ensuing Darkness

1. Robert Service, *Collected Poems of Robert Service.* (G.P.

Putnam's Sons, New York: Penguin Group, 1921), p. 33. From "The Cremation of Sam McGee."

2. Peter M. Leschak, *The Necessity of Darkness*, (Minnesota Conservation Volunteer: State of Minnesota Department of Natural Resources, November-December, 2014), pp. 18-26.

3. Kahlil Gibran, *Jesus: The Son of Man* (Alfred A. Knopf: New York, 1943), p. 171. From "Birbarah of Yammouni."

4. Richard Brookhiser, *"Person of Interest: A Man of Many Fathers"* (Psychology Today: Sussex Publishers, LLC, November 4, 2014), *https://www.psychologytoday.* com/articles/201410/person-interest-man-many-fathers. Richard Brookhiser is the author of the book *Founder's Son: A Life of Abraham Lincoln.*

5. St. John of the Cross, *Dark Night of the Soul*, (Goodreads: https://www.goodreads.com/author/quotes/1911605.

6. St. John of the Cross, *Dark Night of the Soul*, (http://www.ramblingreverend.com/the-dark-night.html. As quoted by Rev. Adam Schell.

7. Jim Brandenburg, *Chased by the Light: A 90-Day Journey*, (Creative Publishing International: Minneapolis, 2001), p. 104. http://www.amazon.com/Chased-Light-90-Day-Journey-Revisited-After/dp/1559718005.

Unfound Riches

Pierre Berton, *Klondike: The Last Great Gold Rush 1896-1899*, (McClelland and Stewart Limited: Toronto, 1972), p. 2.

I Go Up to the North Country to Feel Small

Spike Carlsen, *A Splintered History of Wood*, (Harper Perennial: New York, 2008), pp. Xiii - xiii-xiv.

Raw Beauty

George Marsh, *The Old Canoe*, (Scribner's Magazine: October 1908). As quoted from *Of Time and Place* by Sigurd F. Olson (Alfred A. Knopf: New York, 1982), p. 8.

Dawning Imperatives

1. Pierre Berton, *The Mysterious North: Encounters With the Canadian Frontier* (McClelland & Stewart Inc: Toronto, 1989), p. 22.
2. Joe Walsh, *History of The Eagles: The Story of an American Band* (DVD documentary, Director: Alison Ellwood, Release January 19, 2013.)

Whispers

Elliott Merrick, *True North: A Journey into Unexplored Wilderness, a Memoir*, (North Atlantic Books: Berkeley and Heron Dance Press: North Ferrisburg, 1933), p. 150. Original publisher: C. Scribner's Sons: New York.

Northern Christmas

1. "Yellow lanterns of autumn"; a phrase used by Sigurd F. Olson.

2. Henry David Thoreau, *Walden and Other* Writings, (Barnes & Noble Books: New York, 1993), p. 80.
3. Wikipedia (Wikimedia Foundation, Inc.: https://en.wikipedia.org/wiki/Rowan.)

Arctic Sun

Barry Lopez, *Arctic Dreams*, (Vintage Books, New York: Random House, Inc., 1986), p. 251.

Spring Wait

1. Aldo Leopold, *A Sand County Almanac: And Sketches Here and There* (Oxford University Press, 1939), p. 14. From his article, "Thinking Like A Mountain" as cited from http:// webspace.pugetsound.edu/facultypages/kburnett/readings/ leopold.pdf.
2. John Bates, *A Northwoods Companion: Spring and Summer*, (Manitowish River Press: Mercer, 1997), 43.

SPRING

Jack London, *Jack London Illustrated,* (Avenel Books: New York, 1980), p. 52.

The Ice Fields of March

Margot Morrell and Stephanie Capparell, *Shackleton's Way: Leadership Lessons From the Great Antarctic Explorer*, (Penguin Books: New York, 2001).

The Invisible Hand

1. Paul Rezendes, *Tracking and the Art of Seeing*, (Collins Reference, New York: HarperCollins, 1999), p. 15.
2. *Basic Ojibwe words and phrases,*
www.ojibwe.org/hom/pdf/
3. Source: WorkBook dictionary.
4. Mark Elbroch, *Mammal Tracks & Sign: A Guide to North American Species*, (Stackpole Books: Mechanicsburg, 2003), p. 3.
5. Tom Brown, Jr., *The Tracker* (Penguin Books, 1978,'86).

April Snow

Laurence Gonzales, *Deep Survival: Who Lives, Who Dies, and Why? (W.W. Norton & Company,* New York / London, 2003), p. 239.

Base Camps

Id., p. 284

Stars

1. Robert W. Service. Source unknown.
2. A. Conan Doyle, *The Hound of the Baskervilles*, (Produced by Shreevatsa R, and David Widger, Release date: 2008 / Updated: 2012),
https:/www.gutenberg.org/files/2852/2852-h/2852-h.htm.

Milestones

1. Gordon Livingston, M.D., *Too Soon Old, Too Late Smart* (Marlowe & Company: New York, 2004), p. 87.
2. Jim Brandenburg, *Chased by the Light: A 90-Day Journey*, (Creative Publishing International: Minneapolis, 2001), p. 7. http://www.amazon.com/Chased-Light-90-Day-Journey-Revisited-After/dp/1559718005.

Split Rock: A Tribute to People Aware of their Circumstances

Peter M. Senge, (*The Fifth Discipline: The Art & Practice of the Learning Organization* (Currency Books Doubleday, New York: Random House, Inc., 2006), pp. 131-132.

The Expectancy of the Day

1. Mark Elbroch, *Mammal Tracks & Sign: A Guide to North American Species*, (Stackpole Books: Mechanicsburg, 2003), p. 1.
2. Edwin H. Friedman, *Failure of Nerve: Leadership in the Age of the Quick Fix* (Seabury Books, New York: Church Publishing, Inc., 2007), particularly pp. 29 - 48 for his discussion of imaginative gridlock, the value of chance and the emotional barriers preventing discovery and innovation.
3. Hebrews 11:1, Revised Standard Version: The Holy Bible (Harper and Brothers, New York: 1952)

The Laurentian Divide

Ella Wheeler Wilcox: "The Winds of Fate', (*World Voices,* New York: Hearst's International Library Company, 1916). Cited in www.ellawheelerwilcox.org/poems/pwindsof.htm.

Joy in Common Things

Henry David Thoreau, *Walden and Other* Writings, (Barnes & Noble Books: New York, 1993), p. 173.

SUMMER

Grace Lee Nute, *The Voyageur's Highway: Minnesota's Border Lake Land* (The Minnesota Historical Society: St. Paul, 1941), p. 1.

Switchbacks

Peter M. Senge, (*The Fifth Discipline: The Art & Practice of the Learning Organization* (Currency Books /Doubleday, New York: Random House, Inc., 2006), p. 64.

Kairos Time

Robert Service, *Collected Poems of Robert Service,* (G.P. Putnam's Sons, New York: Penguin Group, 1921), p. 17. From "The Call of the Wild."

Breaking Camp

Don Ian Smith, *Wild Rivers and Mountain Trails*
(Abingdon Press, Nashville / New York, 1972), p. 73. From
"Empty Creel."

Long Portages on Hot Days

Aldo Leopold, *A Sand County Almanac: And Sketches Here
and There* (Oxford University Press, 1939), p. 102. From
"Marshland Elegy."

Solstice

John O'Donohue, *Anam Cara: A Book of Celtic Wisdom*
(Cliff Street Books, New York: an imprint of Harper Collins
Publishers, 1997), p. 81.

Watchfires

Jack London, *Jack London Illustrated,* (Avenel Books: New
York, 1980), p. 65.

Unintended Consequences

Scott Anderson, *Distant Fires: Duluth to Hudson Bay*
(Pfeifer-Hamilton: Duluth, 1990), p. 43.

The Coming of More

1. Sigurd F. Olson, *The Singing Wilderness* (Alfred A. Knopf, New York, 1969), p. 219. From "Landscape of the Universe."

2. Sigurd F. Olson, *Open Horizons* (Alfred A. Knopf, New York, 1976. From "Farewell To Saganaga."

3. Ravi Zacharias, *Why Jesus? Rediscovering His Truth in an Age of Mass Marketed Spirituality*, (FaithWords, New York: Hachette Book Group, 2012), p. xii.

4. William Blake, *The Everlasting Gospel* (The Oxford Book of English Mystical Verse, Nicholson & Lee, eds., 1917), pp. 173-175. Taken from http://www.bartleby.com/236/58.html.

5. The phrase *"deep, irrepressible spiritual hungers"* credited to Ravi Zacharias, *Why Jesus? Rediscovering His Truth in an Age of Mass Marketed Spirituality*, (Faith-Words, New York: Hachette Book Group, 2012).

Blueberry Harvest

Henry David Thoreau, *Walden and Other* Writings, (Barnes & Noble Books: New York, 1993), p. 159.

The Mysterious

1. Aldo Leopold, *A Sand County Almanac: And Sketches Here and There* (Oxford University Press, 1939), p. 194. From "A Taste for Country: The Round River."

2. Robert Service, *Collected Poems of Robert Service,* (G.P.

Putnam's Sons, New York: Penguin Group, 1921), p.3. From "Spell of the Yukon."

3. Stan Rogers, *Fogerty's Cover* (Fogerty's Cove and Cole Harbour Music, released 2013, CD.) From the song "Make and Break Harbour."

4. Mark Steven Johnson (screenplay), *Grumpier Old Men* (*DVD, Warner Brothers/Lancaster Gate, 1995.*)

ACKNOWLEDGMENTS

Many contribute to feelings for wilderness and travel in the canoe country. Campsites are more than fires set up starkly against the gathering darkness. They are about laughter, joie de vivre, shared conversation and time-honored respect.

For me, I'd like to thank the following:

To Sigurd Olson, grandest writer of the North Country, who inspired me and taught me wilderness is more than rocks and trees and stars named in the night sky.

To Robert Service: may we tip a glass to the bard of the North who, in his common poetry, wrote uncommon things.

To Don Ian Smith, rancher, preacher, interpreter of life who could take his experiences in the Salmon River country and make them sing to a young preacher in Saskatchewan.

To Martin Lambert, master story-teller, who took me to

places like Lac LaRonge and the Churchill River system long before I ever got there.

To the brigades of canoeists I have paddled with, sometimes in moonlight, sometimes in choppy water, in waves piling up on joyous August mornings. To those who drove their paddles into the water when we weren't moving against the headwinds, and who persisted.

To my dad who introduced me to camping the day he bought a home-made tent trailer that leaked only when it rained. To my mother who, at age 88, accompanied me over the rocks to sit and watch the day draw down on Lake Superior, who encouraged me.

To those who helped me edit and who offered incisive commentary on this book: to Ham Muus, Thomas Stamps, Steve Molin, Spike Carlsen, Dianne Peterson and Regene Dykstra.

To Vellum for making the process of publishing much more manageable.

To those whose quotes I have used to introduce each chapter. By name, I have acknowledged their contribution and thank them.

To you, the reader, who knows that what I write about is only a fraction of what is out there. May your foot never slip on any rock on the trail. May you have just enough pancake flour to get you home. And may your memories be as rich as mine.

For more information on other blogs, articles and books posted or being considered go to:

birchriverbooks.com

Published: May 2018

NOTE: I am notoriously bad at social media (ask my adult children). My FaceBook account is pretty static. Twitter is a black hole. If you need to contact me, please go to my website mentioned above.

If you enjoyed this book, would you do me the great favor of going to Amazon.com to leave a comment in "Customer Reviews." It's just under this book's title: *Compass Season.* It is the lifeblood of every author to gain such reviews.

BOOK CLUBS

I love the fact friends and acquaintances will get together to expand on ideas of what they have read.

I have prepared a study guide to highlight parts of each chapter if you email me to request this information.

"Books are a uniquely portable magic." – Stephen King

RESOURCES

I have a great list of resources that will help you learn more about a variety of topics. I love these books. I've also included companies I've used to publish this book. It may save you a lot of steps.

I'm finding fantastic new materials, quotations, photographs. It makes sense to move these online where I can update more often.

Visit anytime at birchriverbooks.com.

There is no registration or password needed. I've designed this site to be a bit reminiscent of a visit to the North Country.

Books:

Deep Survival: Who Lives, Who Dies and Why? By

Laurence Gonzales. A great book especially if you love wilderness adventure. Mistakes can be instructive. If you extrapolate conditions, response and lessons learned to your own life. There's a lot that can be applied.

The Singing Wilderness. What a treasure trove of books Sigurd F. Olson has written. This book is among his best. He captures a feeling for the old experience of canoeing back in the 1940's and 50's. It is all there: a scientist's viewpoint, ecology, spirituality seasoned with an ethic and philosophy of the land. Great reading!

Under A Flaming Sky by Daniel James Brown. Not for the faint of heart but descriptive narrative that will keep you wishing you didn't have to get up for work the next morning. Describes the Great Hinckley Firestorm of 1894, its sadness but also places of heroism. The author's wordcraft is impressive in what well could have been a very tedious book.

Collected Poems of Robert Service. Whether your passion is for canoeing, backpacking, rock-climbing, backcountry skiing or armchair adventure, this book should accompany you. His poetry went with miners and tenderfoots deep into the Yukon during the Gold Rush of '98.

By the River of No Return. Don Ian Smith is a rancher, country preacher and an incisive writer. A Christian book but wonderfully insightful and gentle in his approach to faith but also to living. He has other books to that might intrigue you as well.

Recommended for Writing

An Introduction to E-Book Publishing. Go figure! A really clear, straightforward presentation of the ins-and-outs of ebook publishing by SmashWords originator Mark Corker. A great beginner step to take you through the self-publishing process.

Vellum. (https://vellum.pub) Recommended by Creative Penn is good enough for me. Started by guys from Pixar Animation Studios its expertise is in formatting your book so you will like it (not to mention the various sites where it will be placed). The beauty of this is that updating and editing changes can be made at any time - by the author. Gives so much control over the process!

Successful Self-Publishing. Joanna Penn's website is excellent. (https://www.thecreativepenn.com) This site takes it a step further inviting you to walk through her very down-to-earth, practical way of releasing a book into the greater universe.

John A. Bragstad has spent three seasons guiding others by canoe in the Arrowhead region of Minnesota and the Churchill River country of Saskatchewan. He has spent twenty-five years as a licensed Marriage and Family therapist guiding both individuals and couples.

He is trained in cognitive therapy and organizational development and is a certified life coach.

John has resided both in Canada and the United States. He lives happily in Grand Marais, Minnesota with his wife and dog named Jack.

Made in the USA
Middletown, DE
07 April 2019